# GARDENS
## OF PLENTY

# GARDENS OF PLENTY

## MARYLYN ABBOTT

WITH PHOTOGRAPHY BY CLAY PERRY

**TODTRI**

First published in Great Britain in 2001
by Kyle Cathie Limited

This edition published in
the United States in 2002 by
TODTRI Book Publishers
254 West 31st Street
New York, NY10001-2813
Tel: (212) 695-6622
Fax: (212) 695-6984
E-mail: info@todtri.com

Visit us on the web!
www.todtri.com

ISBN 1 -57717-275-2
Text © Marylyn Abbott 2001
Photography © Clay Perry 2001except for pages 10, 11, 13,
14, 15, 16 (Bridgeman Art Library),  12 (Mary Evans Picture
Library) and 17 (Museum of Garden History)
Garden plans © Greg Becker 2001

A CIP catalogue record for this title is available from
the British Library.

Editor: Helen Woodhall
Editorial Assistant: Esme West
Designer: Geoff Hayes
Copy Editor: Helena Attlee
Production: Lorraine Baird & Sha Huxtable
Colour Separations: Colourscan
Printed and bound in Singapore by KHL Printing Co. Pte.Ltd.

For Trisha Priestley
for being there from
17 March to 13 July 1991

# CONTENTS

Opening the pages of the *Sydney Morning Herald*, I was surprised to see a colour photograph of my vegetable garden at Kennerton Green near Mittagong in Australia, a garden that gives me so much true pleasure and where twice a year vegetables, flowers and herbs are planted against walls of fruit to make as fanciful patterns and combinations of riotous colour as I can achieve.

Beneath the photograph an eminent Australian historian was quoted as saying he 'despised the present trend for the potager, an ornamental kitchen garden designed to look pretty as well as to be functional; it was like putting chintz in the kitchen'!

Oh dear, I thought, and then mentally reviewed so many of the worlds great gardens. St Jean de Beauregarde and Villandry in France, Kasteel Hex in the Netherlands and Hatfield House in England passed in review with their virtuoso potagers, then the thousand of small gardens where a few fruit trees, vegetables, flowers and herbs are by necessity planted in controlled formation to form the simplest and most pleasing *jardin potagers*. It was then that I did not feel quite so shattered, as I liked the company I kept.

I am sure the gentleman was harking back to the vegetable garden of his Australian childhood and its remembered remnants of a Victorian past, for I too remember them as very dull affairs hidden as far as possible 'down the back' and fenced or hedged often by some very inhospitable vegetation, impenetrable hedges of rough lemons, with rapier sharp thorns to instantly puncture rubber tires, or tangled stands of prickly pear, a flat cactus that could have come from an inquisitors imagination. Our vegetable garden had just rabbit proof fencing behind which two rows of every ordinary vegetable was laid out in dusty isolation, two lines each of carrots, cabbages, parsnips and iceberg lettuce, the precious water dribbled every evening directly onto their roots from a black, snake-like hose. The paths of natural gravel were home to thriving bull ant nests, the ants 6 vicious inches of pure pain, and a rusty sheet of corrugated iron lain across the compost heap completed an extremely functional picture.

Flower gardens were strictly for company, fanning out from the house around a lawn kept emerald green whatever the cost, from where fruit trees in the adjoining orchard were viewed but rarely visited. This was my concept of how gardens were designed, an impression enhanced in a much grander manner by my first visit to English gardens, where lakes, ponds, terraces and sweeping lawns bordered by herbaceous beds surrounded majestic houses that welcomed visitors, while the vegetable garden was not to be seen but hidden behind forbidding walls, the gates tightly locked.

That same trip I passed through the door of a great chateau in France onto a vast terrace, and in one sweep

# INTRODUCTION

of the eye I registered an enormous pattern of colours, a formal design where precise rows of plants of different textures created the most extraordinary garden. Here garden apartheid was abolished and segregated plants were intermingled, creating a magic carpet for me to walk from one way of life to another.

The great potager of Villandry and the tiny village gardens planted in simple order that press close to the roads in rural France must have dusted their magic on hundreds of visitors, for now gardens inspired by this enthralling interpretation of an older French tradition have been made across the world. The converted, like me, have found many advantages to planting in this manner; regardless of what seed packets, say I do believe that plants grow stronger planted closer together, and it is much more fun to try and expel white fly by growing those brilliant gold sun spots, the French marigolds than spraying out a deadly concoction.

Over the years, the potager has been adapted to every conceivable climate and geography. It has embraced 1,500 years of change, absorbing first the plants that reached Europe from the Americas in the fifteenth century, and now a fashionable range of Asian vegetables, herbs and fruits. Only a decade ago these were basically unknown to cooks in Europe, America and Australia, but today they look perfectly at home beside ruffled parsley and prosaic cabbages.

This is a book for those who wish to ignore the puritanical, Anglo-Saxon view of vegetable patches as places of virtuous toil, and to allow Gaelic frivolity into the garden, allowing flowers and sensuous herbs to cohabit. It will take you on a journey of discovery through three continents, where individual gardeners have made their own interpretations of the potager

tradition, using plants that would be unrecognisable to the ninth-century French monk hoeing in his garden.

The northern European potager that we glimpse in medieval woodcuts and manuscripts was enclosed behind protecting walls of wood or stone. The south-facing wall of the garden was often devoted to the cultivation of stone fruits, which need as much warmth as possible, and espaliered apples and pears ripened against the other walls. In Mediterranean lands, the walls could play host to every variety of citrus. A modern garden planted just a few years ago adapted the medieval blueprint to a tropical climate. The garden was planted with mango trees espaliered along wires and hedges of flamboyantly coloured hibiscus.

As populations grow and land becomes a luxury in the urban environment, smart young gardeners have adapted the potager to the smallest of city spaces. It appears as a table-top garden on a roof terrace or confined to an oil drum — a useful solution for a mobile population.

Wherever I go, I find gardeners who treasure the potager style. Every garden is a new experience because each gardener has found a unique way of creating beautiful and productive patterns in beds or containers, urging flowers, vegetables, fruits and herbs into designs that respect the available space and make the happiest use of it.

Potagers are gardens for every season. When the dead hand of winter claims the bare earth and the first snow-fall covers the garden, it is more beautiful than ever. The geometric patterns become traceries, like the carved grill of the confessional or the shadow pattern of a cathedral window, and we know, as the monks did of old, that the eye of God is on these gardens, and we are blessed.

*I am the true vine, and my Father is the husband man.*

*Every branch in me that beareth not fruit he taketh away: and every branch that beareth fruit, he purgeth it, that it may bring forth more fruit.*

JOHN 15: 1–2

# CHAPTER 1
## MEDIEVAL CLUES

The history of the potager can be pieced together from clues and fragments of information woven into tapestries or tucked away in medieval manuscripts, lines of poetry, or even in the records of medieval man's legal disputes. A Latin school book for Aelfric's class of AD995 lists 200 known plants and trees. Another chance snippet is King William Rufus' pretext for viewing a promising Saxon princess in 1092. He claimed that the purpose of his visit was 'to see the roses and other flowering herbs' in Romsey Abbey – thus recording the plants grown in the garden at

the time. (History relates that this botanical subterfuge did not work. Edith, safely concealed in her habit, passed by unnoticed.)

An enchanting poem written by Walafrid Strabo, a Benedictine monk over a thousand years ago, strikes a cord with every gardener Strabo writes of weeding his nettle-infested courtyard, to transform it into a garden of herbs, flowers, fruit and vegetables.

*But this little patch which lies facing east*
*In the small courtyard before my door*
*Was full of nettles. All over...*
*So I put it off no longer. I set to with my mattock*
*And dug up the sluggish ground. From their embrace...*

*And God said, Let the earth bring forth grass, the herb yielding seed, and the fruit tree yielding fruit after his kind, whose seed is in itself, upon the earth: and it was so.*

*And the earth brought forth grass, and herb yielding seed after his kind, and the tree yielding fruit, whose seed was in itself, after his kind: and God saw that it was good.*

GENESIS 1: 11-12

As the first millennium loomed, Europe's only unifying force was the church and church Latin the only common language. Travel between the religious foundations provided a thread of communication. How many of imperial Rome's traditions were preserved behind monastic walls is debatable, but a returning Roman would have recognised the four-square grid of the monastery garden and the roses, myrtle and box bushes often to be found there.

Roman culture had absorbed the more ancient 'paradise' gardens of Mesopotamia. These, like Roman peristyle gardens, were protected by walls and consisted of a cruciform arrangement of paths and watercourses. Radiating from a central pool or a fine palm tree, channels would cut the lush garden into four squares representing the four continents. The tree at the centre of the Christian medieval garden in southern Europe could be the olive, symbol of God's mercy, or a cypress to symbolise peace. Further north it might be an apple tree, reminding the devout of Adam's fall from grace. Under Christian influence, the central pool or water fountain often represented the four rivers of Paradise: Pison, Geon, Tigress and Euphrates, and the axis represented Christ's cross viewed from above by God.

Although not a single medieval garden survives, a ninth-century plan for a monastery garden was found at St Gall in Switzerland. It is very plain with utilitarian, square beds, the only ornamentation a cross centred in the orchard cemetery. The plan suggests that the beds were 1.5m (5ft) long, with a single plant species allotted to each plot. The paths between the beds were 1.2m (4ft) wide.

Medieval gardens can be glimpsed behind the achingly beautiful Madonnas and swan-necked ladies of illuminated manuscripts. They are walled enclosures where busy gardeners tend small, precisely squared beds. Roses that can be identified as varieties of *R. Gallica* and *R. Alba* escape from walls of stakes, trellis and woven willow. Fine fruit trees are espaliered along supports or walls in these idealised cameos of medieval life.

Walls were a vital defence against marauding man and beast. In *The Merchant's Tale*, Chaucer refers to stone walls in the old knight's garden – obviously an up-market retreat.

*He made a gardin, walled al with stoon;*
*So fair a gardin woot I nowher noon'*
THE MERCHANT'S TALE

*The Nuns Priest Tale* is set in a fairly ordinary garden:

*A yearde she hadde, enclosed al aboute*
*With stickkes and a drye ditch without.*

If a wooden or woven fence would not keep unwelcome visitors at bay, a boggy ditch might. An absolute palisade against man and beast is described as an interplanting of 'Hazel trees, gooseberry bushes, white and red pepper trees, eglantine, brambles, wood binde, the wilde vines, both the hollies, elder trees, intermingled now and then with white thorne, wild apple trees, service trees (*sorbus domestica*) medlars and olives.'

A twelfth-century Burgundian monk described the potager at his abbey in the following words:

*. . . within the walls of the cloister, there is a wide level ground, here there is an orchard, with a great many different fruit trees, quite like a small wood. It is close to the infirmary and very comforting to the brothers. Where the orchard leaves off the garden begins, divided into several beds or (better still) cut up by little canals, which though of standing water, do flow more or less. The water fulfils the double purpose of nourishing the fish and watering the vegetables*

Many Classical texts, and a selection of more recent ones were used by monks and noblemen when planning a new garden. A fortunate abbot might have a copy of Pliny the Elder's *Natural History* in his library. Inherited from the Classical world, this remained one of the main sources of reference on plants for many centuries. Another first-century work was the *Herbal de Materia Medica*, written by a Greek physician called Dioscorides. It was lost to Europe until it came back by a roundabout route, translated from the Greek to Arabic and then to Latin. It listed 500 plants, their properties, uses and methods of harvesting. The Latin poem 'Macer Floridus' listed eighty plants. It was translated into English and was very widely used in monasteries. The great Charlemagne, concerned for the health and welfare of his people, decreed that seventy-three herbs and sixteen fruit and nut trees must be grown in official lands.

In the *Domesday Book* of 1086, the Normans found that ninety per cent of English people lived directly off the land. Gardens were a vital source of food and medicine for medieval peasant, priest and noble alike, and also of solace and joy in an often cold and disease ridden world.

English men began to write about plants as a source of pleasure in the twelfth century. Alexander Neckham, the young foster brother of Richard the Lion Heart, was the first. He wrote *Die Naturis Rerum*, a work devoted to trees, herbs and flowers for adorning the garden. Bartholomaeus Glanville compiled an encyclopaedia with a book devoted to plants.

By the thirteenth century, pleasure gardens were definitely on the agenda. Albertus Magnus, who wrote *De Vegetabilibus et Plantis* and Pietro de' Crescenzi's *Liber Ruralium Commodorum*, could perhaps be blamed for our fetish for over-indulged lawns. The fault lies with him when he claims that 'the sight is in no way so pleasantly refreshed as by fine and close grass kept short'!

London-based Henry Daniel, a Dominican monk and doctor, wrote a very precise herbal, including local and imported plants and citing all the major classical herbalists and medieval plant encyclopaedias.

The many uses and properties attributed to herbs, vegetables, fruit and flowers make enchanting reading for the twenty-first-century gardener:

Previous page, from left: A mural painting in Pompeii; 'Sowing the Seed' by Pietro de Crescenzi in *Le Rustican*, 1460, which shows one plant variety in each bed and an arched tunnel for training cooling vines or fruit trees.

Opposite: 'Construction of a Garden House with Formal Gardens and Landscape in the Background' in *Livre des Prouffits Champetres*, a fifteenth-century manuscript.

Left: A wall painting of a dove in a garden by a fountain, Pompeii, first century AD.

Rue (*Ruta graveolens*) is a beautiful, lacy, aqua-blue herb which can be cut to form cushions or create decorative edges to beds. We learn in a delightful verse from Adam in Eden 1657 that:

*Rue maketh chaste and preserveth sight,*
*Infuseth wit, and Fleas doth put to Flight!!*

Rue was also thought to deter adders! Rosemary was used as a spice and could cure a range of physical and psychological ills. According to thirteenth-century Queen Philippa's mother:

*[it] doth away evil spirits and suffereth not*
*to dreame fowle dreemes...*

Below: Many medieval illustrations show raised beds surrounded by 'wattling', a simple weaving of local saplings. Here the great golden squash at le Prieuré Notre Dame d'Orsan revel in this recreation of a medieval gardening technique.

Some plants have enduring properties. Liquorice (*Glycrrhiza glabra*) for example, is still used to treat coughs and colds, hoarseness and catarrh.

Poisonous plants were well identified; monkshood, foxglove and henbane often grew in a locked enclosure within the monastery garden, along with the sedative and hallucinogenic plants. The medieval slimmer was told to take savory (*Satureja montana* and *S. hortensis*) and thyme was used as a hangover cure.

During the Middle Ages, vegetables were of the most basic kind; peas and beans, cabbage, leeks, onions and rhubarb were used to treat 'wamblings of the gut', convulsions, cramps and sciatica. Medieval carrots were either purple or yellow and, along with parsnips and turnips, they were the dietary staples. Garlic was grown, like onions, in every vegetable patch, and both of them were used to add dash to very boring meals. Chaucer's repulsive summonier must have stunk:

*Garlic he loved and onions too, and leeks,*
*And drinking strong red wine till all was hazy.*

A clove of garlic held in the mouth was said to prevent plague, or perhaps the smell just kept every one at bay, reducing the spread of the disease.

In addition to their use as food, flavour and fragrance, flowers were attributed medical and magical properties. Essential in the life of the church, the rose symbolised Mary and scattered roses were the gift of the Holy Spirit. Garlands of red roses were made for Corpus Christi and The Feast of the Martyrs. The lily signified Mary's purity, its golden anthers the light of her soul. Lilies were also thought to cure scalds and tumours of the genitals. Violets symbolised Mary's humility and were used to calm fevers, headaches and carbuncles and to flavour sauces.

Flowers in garlands, wreaths and crowns also had a more practical purpose. The smells of medieval life must have been horrid and fresh flowers provided natural perfumes. Flowers were tossed among the rushes on the floor and roses and violets were used in early versions of essential oils to mask the unpleasant smells of everyday life.

By the first millennium, many gardens contained a small enclosure or outdoor room, set apart from the orchard, meadow, productive gardens, fish-ponds and canals. This 'herber' or pleasure garden was set aside for the abbott, prioress, or ladies of the court. The exquisite illustration in the *Hours of the Duke of Burgundy* shows virginal Emilia, untouchable in her rose-walled herber. The illustration shows us exactly what a turf seat looked like, and also includes the ubiquitous vine-covered arbour. The jewelled 'Madonna of the Rose Arbour' (c.1440) sits on a turf bench studded with daisies, violets, red clover and strawberries, surrounded by a squared arch of climbing red and white roses and tall white lilies (*Lilium regale*), symbolising Mary, the centre of the Church. The garden, at the centre of the church world, was a paradise, safe from the dark, wild world beyond.

The fifteenth-century German painting of 'The Garden of Paradise' shows ribbon beds filled with borage, campion, cowslip, daisy, purple flag iris, hollyhock, Madonna lily, lychnis, peony, periwinkle, sweet rocket, sage, snowdrops and strawberries.

Right: 'A Garden' by Johan Walter in *Florilege de Nasseau-Idstein*, 1660, which depicts a Renaissance garden, still protected and enclosed, but now devoted wholly to pleasure and display.

As the world became a more secure place, and man could be diverted from mere survival, the garden became more complex. There were highly decorated tubs and urns of flowers, and trees of different species were clipped into mop heads, parasols and three-tiered balls.

From the words of the poet Geoffrey Chaucer, we glean that the late medieval garden had become a lively and very human place:

*Hoom to myn hous ful swiftly I me spedde.*
*To goon to reste, and erly for to ryse,*
*To seen this flour to sprede, a I devyse.*
*And, in a litel herber that I have,*
*That benched was on turves fresshe y-grave,*
*I bad men sholde me my couche make...*

By the sixteenth century, people of power and wealth had divided their gardens into different areas. The traditional four-square grid now became the frame for *parterres de broderie*, fountains played from elaborate ponds and fruit trees, flowers and vegetables were partitioned off into separate spaces. The change was a gradual one, but by the 1590's a fresco of the Villa Medici at Castello in Italy showed walled gardens of square beds still planted with medieval favourites and separated from a central, formal garden. Other, separate areas were laid down as meadows, or planted with trees.

In France, the gardens of Diane de Poitiers at Chenonceaux were laid out in 1550 as a large rectangle with plantings that were most definitely that of the *jardin potager*. Archival records confirm this observation. The garden was subdivided by two wide, cross-axis paths that created four rectangles. It was then divided again into twenty-four equal plots within large ramparts. The site was laid out with knots and a labyrinth and planted with trees of plum, cherry, pear and dwarf apple, sweet-smelling violets, lilies and musk roses, rows of sprouts, currants, artichokes, cabbages, onions, melons and peas. This was a mixture as heady as the lady herself. Within ten years, however, Catherine de Medici, having ousted her husband's mistress, redesigned the garden, imposing a more formal, Renaissance planting and using the site to stage marvellous entertainments of fireworks, water fêtes and masques

The seventeenth-century Potager Le Roi at Versailles is a monumental example of a segregated garden that has been wonderfully preserved. Beyond the grand allées and vistas of Le Nôtre, it stands behind massive grey walls, in the shadow of the Cathedral of St Louis. It is so well hidden from the palace that the many thousands of tourists that team through the forecourt are unaware of its existence. Arriving at the garden from a side street is like walking down into a double-walled pit. The space is subdivided into numerous rectangular gardens, all espaliered with ripening fruits around a central formal design.

Victorian Britons wanted their kitchen gardens completely concealed from sight. They were enclosed within walls of brick or stone and then often screened again with a hedge or shrubbery. Sometimes, the vegetable garden was sited a mile from the kitchen door, ensuring absolute separation of its smells and activities from polite society. Firmly stripped of their magic and mythology, frivolous flowers were excluded from these gardens of industrial productivity, where a pause for contemplation or meditation would have been grounds for instant dismissal.

Has the fascination with the potager garden been a

rebellion against these monolithic segregated gardens, a desire to return to a more natural association between man, his plants and animals? Is today's 'potager' garden simply a romantic mixture of the medieval kitchen garden, the herbs of the physic garden, details gleaned from a herbal and any other medieval elements it pleases us to include? The plants we choose represent a mixture amassed over 2,000 years and happily blended to make any number of delicious recipes for soup or potage.

The appeal of the 'French style', as it is thought of today, has been exploited by gardeners worldwide. What was probably just a very grubby monastery yard has been invigorated and energised. The fragments of medieval manuscripts that we try to interpret may be completely inaccurate, idealised versions of the truth, made by artist monks. Has the tradition been perfectly maintained in European village gardens, or is this just a case of a urban society making another, so-called rediscovery?

Above: Ordered horticulture with large glass houses for continuous food production in the kitchen garden of a country house in northern England, 1915.

# CHAPTER 2
## A MEDIEVAL
## INTERPRETATION

My search to understand the evolution of the potager began with le Prieuré Notre Dame d'Orsan. On a hot summer's day I entered a rolling landscape of unkempt hedges bordering untilled fields. Nothing was happening, the villages seemed deserted in the afternoon light and as I looked in vain for grazing animals, a gap in the hedge appeared. In it stood a Romany woman against the backdrop of an encampment. It was a timeless encounter, but before the black magic of the Berry could take over, the French Air Force screamed overhead, dragging me back with a thud into the twenty-first century.

In the eleventh century there was a monk who sought out carnal frustration in order to strengthen his will. He came here, to the centre of France, and founded a priory. Almost as though the Berry witches resented its presence, the priory endured a turbulent history and was finally dissolved during the French Revolution.

Over twelve years ago, two young Parisian architects came to this valley. Sonia Lesot and Patrice Taravella were captivated by the mystery of the place and the potential of its remaining buildings, and they resolved to make a monastic garden in the great courtyard.

At an emotional level this is still a medieval garden of biblical inspiration, but above all it is an idealised space created by two successful young people who turned their backs on their world, which was centred on Parisian design. As Patrice says: 'the wish to garden, like the wish to

# LE PRIEURÉ NOTRE
# DAME D'ORSAN, FRANCE

Opposite: Woven sapling edges support beds of thyme topped by a young olive tree.

Above: Fruits, flowers and herbs surround a maze of trained plum trees.

Left: Hornbeam trees trained to cover a new dividing screen, and forcing pots made from twigs and saplings create exciting texture below the rhubarb leaves.

Below: Central to the garden is the fountain, its four water jets representing the rivers of the Bible; part of the garden's enduring delight is its trellis and shapes made from natural materials.

grow, corresponds to a profound need to appropriate a fragment of the cosmos. It involves taking the time to rediscover, in situ, the biological pace'.

What remains of the priory is not beautiful in the architectural sense. The massive, solid buildings create austere, functional spaces, designed to focus the mind on God. The garden is entered through iron-bound priory gates and a stone porch, where, laid out as a rigid, geometric configuration, each compartment is devoted to an aspect of the medieval garden.

The first parterre is dominated by the surrounding buildings. The very utilitarian nature of the grey, plastered walls may have influenced the design of these first gardens. They consist of large, simple, square beds planted with wheat, beans and cabbages in rotation. I saw the garden when the wheat was golden and ready to be harvested. Already, two crosses of St David had been cut across the wide squares of rippling wheat, enforcing the message that this grass is 'the staff of life' and that wheaten bread becomes the body of Christ.

The beds of wheat are reminiscent of the great wheat parterres designed by Fernando Caruncho in Spain. Caruncho's inspiration is rooted in Europe's medieval past. In *Gardens of the Future* by Gordon Taylor and Guy Cooper, he is quoted as saying 'In order to travel to the future, it is necessary to walk towards the pure clarity of the past'.

Here the garden is enclosed by a green cloister of hornbeam, interlaced with *Wisteria sinensis* and *Clematis montana*. Where the four central paths cross, there is a fountain 'reflecting the harmony of creation and foreshadowing the paradise lying before the monk if he gave himself to divine love'.

The grapes for the other element of the ritual of Holy Communion is celebrated by the clear water. I saw white Chenin grapes ripening over wooden rails grown again in a garden divided by a four-square grid.

Crunching down the beautifully maintained gravel paths, brushing against lavenders designed to be trodden on so that they will release their oil and perfume, the path leading towards the orchard intersects with allies of gooseberries, raspberries, blackcurrants, redcurrants, blueberries and strawberries, carefully protected from flying predators. Each fruit bed is enclosed by apple and pear trees espaliered in a variety of different styles. Some trees have been trained with two upright branches as Us on either side of the main trunk known as U-shaped Palmette. Others are criss-crossed in a diamond pattern, a simple horizontal cord, or a superimposed bilateral cord, where two trees of different heights have their branches trained at different levels. The sideways oblique cord and the curve upon curved branch of the cord style are also displayed.

The tiny pears were just forming on the horizontal cords. Already they were captured inside glass bottles., where before long someone would be asking that age-old question: 'how did such a large pear get into a Poire William bottle?' To keep the forming pear cool in its glass prison, beautifully made twig witches hats were placed on the bottom of each bottle, casting a gentle shade.

The central path is laid to grass as it crosses the orchard. Here, twenty-three varieties of apple rise from a flowery meadow, contained by a flowering fence of hawthorn, lilac, quince and plum.

Walking from the orchard, the high, green walls of the plum-tree maze conceal the kitchen garden. The hedge uses various varieties of plum, including 'Saint Catherine', golden greengage, Alsace and the Nancy cherry plum. It is difficult to espalier the small, dense, green leaves, but the leaf walls make a green fabric – another texture among many. The enclosure creates isolation from the world outside, encouraging spiritual thoughts.

Like all good pilgrims to paradise, I was soon lost in the kitchen maze. I could hear the sound of clipping in the distance and so I called out for help. A voice answered, 'If you follow the beds of plants brought to Europe from America you will not find paradise. Follow the plants of medieval Europe and you will complete your journey!'

Orsan's labyrinth of paradise passes many beautiful concepts, such as lush rhubarb rising above cylindrical twig forcers of woven chestnut, vine and willow. Long shelves of twigs have been laid on wooden frames, each supporting a single squash plant, which creeps its way along, the ripening vegetables like golden-green ornaments protected from ground damp and mildew.

Herbs, flowers and vegetables grow in profusion. Many prayers may have been said over a trinity of tripods covered in rampant morning glory above tall stands of poppies and larkspur with strawberries at their feet. Waving fronds of angelica, fennel and asparagus, with the architectural artichoke surrounded by trailing nasturtiums, and bold clumps of chives, coriander, basil, tarragon and parsley, are interspersed with Irish bells (*Moluccella laevis*), parsnips, carrots and chard.

Above: a rustic shelter covers a tender herb from sun or frost

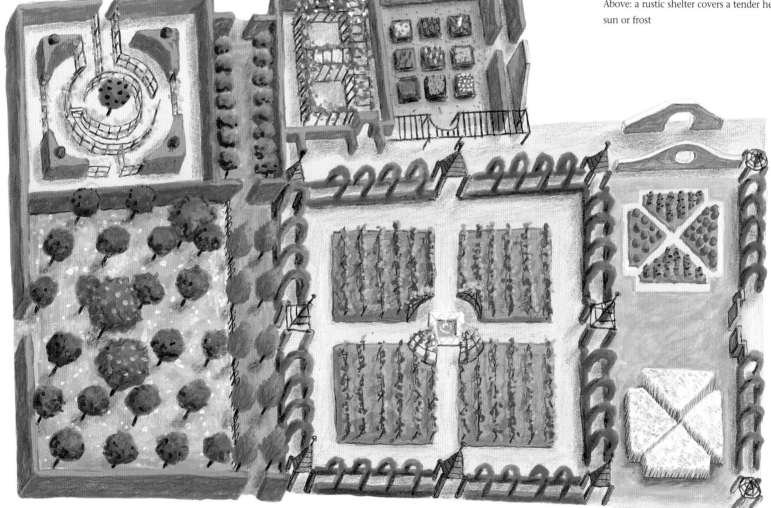

Eventually, on a road of wooden slab, one reaches paradise. Here a trained apple tree in the centre of the green lawn creates an umbrella of shade over the round, woven-chestnut benches where the weary pilgrim can rest at the journey's end.

From Gothic windows set in covered cloisters of chestnut saplings, supporting walls of green horn beans, dozens of climbing roses intertwine. There are the white roses 'Aimée Vibert', 'Madame Alfred Carrière', 'Albéric Barbier', 'Mrs Herbert Stevens' and 'Lamarque' mixed with pink varieties such as 'New Dawn', 'Pierre de Ronsard', 'Albertine' and 'Paul Noel'. In all, twenty varieties intermingle to create two small cloisters. Square beds are planted with all the flowers dedicated to Mary – roses, roses and more roses, lilies, violets and iris – the medieval vision of the church with the Madonna at its centre.

In this totally inspirational garden it is often difficult to decide where Christian symbolism finishes and the magic circle begins. Tall, rustic supports made of fanciful twists of willow could come from a wizard's workshop. One giant sunflower stands like a sun trained through a hoop, seen atop trellises of tomatoes with green and red cabbages crossed at their feet.

Use of wood in the garden creates a lasting impression. It appears woven into walls, tall arcades, benches and the edges of beds. It is used to create strangely shaped plant supports, birds' trapezes and shelters for tender plants. These structures are woven from all that the local forest can provide. Long, pliant lengths of hazel, willow and chestnut, twigs, branches and grasses are reincarnations of some long-gone wood spirit that has evolved into the Christian message woven into every aspect of the garden.

At the centre of the garden lie nine squares arranged in groups of three. They are built up above ground level and surrounded by chestnut fencing. The design pays homage to the number three as it appears in Greek and Christian mythology, representing the Christian Trinity and the Greek phases of the moon. Shining like great golden moons, pumpkins ripen in the beds at eye level, their great wide leaves making a dark underworld for three old women, Selene, Aphrodite and Hecate.

Across the garden, in what was once the infirmary, the individual beds of simples are set out. I expected the French equivalent of the fictional Brother Cadfael to join me here, intent on harvesting some of the eighty-eight plants in the garden and the tender herbs, here sheltered by the broom and willow, that it was decreed should be planted in each abbey. Instead of Cadfael, Patrice appeared, twenty-first-century smart in black polo neck and well-cut trousers to talk about his Priory Restaurant. A glass of chilled white wine tempted me away from the garden.

The garden at le Prieuré Notre Dame d'Orsan is a marriage between medieval simplicity, good gardening and French sophistication. For me this is the haute couture of gardening, that mystical union of style and harmony rarely seen without God's blessing on each element.

Opposite and left: Natural materials are decoratively shaped to introduce the symbolism of magic, the church and even love throughout the garden.

# CHAPTER 3

# GRAND INTERPRETATIONS

The words privilege, power and pretension loom over never-ending rows of salad vegetables, lines of old roses, leviathan delphiniums and flashy summer annuals. At Easter blossoms cling to innumerable boughs of espaliered fruit trees on the high walls, beside mono-grammed arches and turrets of grey slate, that surround the grand potagers of France.

Many of the gardens I saw were struggling for survival, the latest row of vegetables already engulfed by weeds. In one place a solitary gardener could be seen, moving a wooden barrow of stakes. In another, a student apatheti-cally picked up a hoe. These were the sole remnants of long-departed teams of gardeners. In many cases, only half

of the enclosed space was still tended, but nevertheless, traces of a lavish past could still be found. In some gardens the appearance of beds honoured a medieval layout, while the methods used for training fruit trees, the pollarding techniques, the supports made for tall or fragile plants and the ingenious devices for trellising could all have been drawn directly from the pages of a medieval manuscript. Many of these skills, long forgotten in anglicised gardens, survive in a tradition unbroken since the Middle Ages.

The best potagers in France are still picture perfect, and they are revered by gardeners all over the world. If we are truly to understand the ethos of the *jardin potager*, it is essential that we visit France's grand potager gardens.

# VILLANDRY

This book had its genesis one late afternoon nearly thirty years ago. I pushed open a door in the side wall at Villandry, and found myself looking down on to a terrace that appeared to be covered by a giant patchwork quilt.

When one looks closely for the first time at an Amish quilt, it takes time to realise that the tiny, complex shapes are made of simple strips of printed cotton arranged in intricate geometric patterns. In just the same way, I did not immediately understand what I saw at Villandry. There were nine geometric parterres. As I gazed at them, I slowly realised that they were not filled with exotic blooms, but instead contained nothing more unusual than an everyday collection of vegetables and over-bright annuals, immaculately tended in a precision grid.

I was smitten. As a novice gardener without a great knowledge of plants, I realised that the potager style had something unique to offer me. Working on a small scale, I could immediately create something of beauty from these simple plants that encompassed my limited gardening vocabulary, the rigid pattern offering the outlines of a colouring-in book

Dr Joachin Carvallo, the designer of the potager at Villandry, came to this immense undertaking not as a horticulturist but as a scientist. The sixteenth-century château was in a very dilapidated state when he bought it in 1906, beginning a programme of major repairs that included the removal the totally inappropriate *jardin anglais*, all lawns and dotted beds, from around the château.

Carvallo studied Jacques Androuet du Cerceau's sixteenth -century engravings of the royal châteaux of Blois and

Previous page: Inspirational parterres at Villandry and a pink border at St Jean de Beauregard.

Below: Standard roses punctuate the formal design.

Chambord and the terraced gardens of Amboise. He also read descriptions of Classical gardens and the monastic gardens of the Middle Ages. His research led to the reawakening of his dormant Catholic faith, bringing him to a belief in the hierarchical social order, with its pyramid of descending classes. These beliefs were reflected in his new gardens, where parterres on a level with the rooms of the château were designed to symbolise courtly love. Prosaic fruits, vegetables and simple flowers were planted at the lowest level of his personal pyramid of the plant world.

Caravallo knew the simple gardens of the Loire villages, where vegetables, fruit, flowers and herbs were grown in carefully tended geometric plots. A dovecote, a few hens and a cow or goat tethered beside the lake or forest completed the picture, and he saw the spirit of the practical, monastery garden preserved in these.

The Villandry gardens are not historically accurate. They are a wonderful confection of Medieval and Renaissance gardening ideas, ornamented with Italianate detail. They are, above all, a physical manifestation of the wishes of one remarkable man. Carvallo wanted to create a spiritual garden, incorporating a square, central pool as the axis of each central cross. The repeated cruciform design and prominent use of roses are all redolent of Medieval mysticism. However, the design owes more to Renaissance engravings than Medieval ones, as it is outlined by tightly-clipped box hedges and enclosed first by fences of espaliered pears and then by high stone walls topped with clipped lime trees.

Like an enormous banquet table prepared for a feast, each parterre is an individual work of art. Each of the potager's nine geometric patterns is totally unique. The only curves to appear in the design are four corner bowers that link the pattern together, shaded arches near cooling

Below: Globular-shaped trees of ripening pears and immaculate rows of vegetables and flowers.

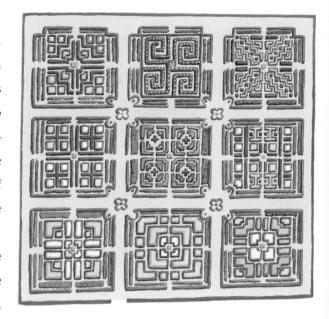

water and the curved leaf or petal within a connected bed.

The giant pattern of the Villandry potager garden convinces the visitor that perfection is possible in this world. The confined, low-growing plants seem not to catch the wind as trees do, which means that there is a stillness here not found in other gardens. So controlled is the atmosphere that even the vertical leaves of an entire bed of leeks seem to grow together, in unison. The maturing kale appears to pause, so that the plants can bolt in concert.

Villandry's gardens bear no relationship to any of the other great, green gardens of France. It takes time for the eye to adjust and absorb the true vibrancy of each static, green pattern and the mass of plants that first capture the imagination. To the anglicised gardener it comes as a surprise to see roses among the onions and salvias beside the peas, and the textures created by the green vegetables present another surprise. The miles of lettuce plants, 29,000 in all, are particularly striking, planted in precise, immaculately tilled lines, like carpet runners of multi-layered leaf texture. There might be as many as 4,000 of the green and dark red lettuce 'Grenoble Red', edged with 300 'Romaine' lettuce. The dark red 'Rondo Batavia' might be co-ordinated with 3,600 'Floreal Dorée de Printemps' in repeated beds, creating a perfectly balanced pattern that M. Pierre Lapin would consider a heavenly blanket.

Green cabbages, 3,500 in all, with veins in tones of blue, red and green, are planted in early spring, along with plugs of onions and the seeds of peas and radishes. As many as 15kg of broad beans and lentils are sown, adding to the incredible statistics of this garden. Among the 20,000 annuals needed for the potager each spring, there are 3,832 brash and brilliant salvia plants, 2,000 *Verbena* 'Verona' and 3,440 blinding, yellow French marigolds. The deep

Below: Seen from the bottom terrace the château at Villandry commands a grandstand view of the world's most famous vegetable garden.

lipstick-pink *Nicotiana* 'Rogue' that often edges an entire design is ordered in batches of 4,920.

On 15 June the spent spring plants go out and a new summer planting is made. This can include coloured chards, celery, aubergines and further mid-season flowers such as petunias and hot-coloured dahlias to give a long sunburst of colour well into the autumn.

New experiments are always taking place at Villandry, using vegetables and annuals of traditional and modern varieties. The aim of the experiments is always to achieve the most successful combinations of texture and colour. Plants sometimes fail here, as they will in any garden. Approximately ten per cent of each batch of seedlings is held back and potted on. These plants are kept in the wings as replacements in case of disaster.

Tall wooden doors separate the service buildings from the extraordinary tranquillity of the garden. Here, cathedral-sized spaces swallow up the serried trays of plugs and seedlings disgorged from shining pantechnicons in the courtyard. Patrice Chauday, Head Gardener, works in an

Left: Confined by the exact geometry summer cosmos fills the parterres that stretch along the upper terrace.

office that is the image of tidy efficiency with watercolour plans showing the planting for season upon season. The decorative detail of these plans transforms them into works of art that would be considered highly desirable as drawing room paintings by many a gardener.

To achieve the extraordinary standard of horticulture visitors expect from Villandry, traditional methods of fertilisation are used. The decorative crops are rotated over a four-year period in soils made from ninety-five percent organic material. This is a combination of sterilised leaf mould, compost made from old vegetables and farmyard manure. The maturing plants are watered with a liquid fertiliser. Nine full-time gardeners along with seasonal staff and horticultural students laboriously weed the entire garden by hand, so that the roots of the box hedges enclosing every bed will not be disturbed. The garden is still owned by the Carvallo family, who oversee every detail.

This garden, more than any other, has unleashed the French potager style on the world. It has opened our eyes to the beauty of the French village garden that inspired Carvallo, and it has awakened our interest in decorative vegetables. As a result, an incredible selection of plants are now available to us at home, many of them unheard of a few decades ago.

So compelling is the fascination of the kitchen garden that it dominates all of Villandry's other gardens: the four ornamental parterres dedicated to love, the parterre that symbolises music, the water garden, the herb garden and the maze. When people speak of Villandry they speak of the kitchen garden, repeating the delightful and incorrect romantic myths that have inspired a new generation of vegetable gardeners, persuading them to cut loose and be boldly adventurous, to redesign and interplant just as the heart dictates.

Below: Ruby red chard and nicotiana in the annual pink border.

Opposite: Grape vines escape from their home behind the cutting beds.

# ST JEAN DE
# BEAUREGARDE, FRANCE

The last of the sprawling suburbs of Paris were contained by fields of ripe wheat. These were crossed by a narrow ribbon of tarmac that appeared to be racing towards a distant woodland, dressed in the deep, shady green of mid-summer. The road served to draw the eye from the heat of the fields to the cool gloom of the woods.

Tall, noble gates dwarfed a tiny gate house and allowed a shaft of light to break through the trees and on to the gravel drive, leading the way to the forecourt of this most intimidating and impressive of châteaux.

In the filtered light an imaginary scene flashed before my eyes. For a split second I saw the Paris mob with malev-olent, flaming torches, straining at the gate, raging at this elegant symbol of the aristocracy. Then I imagined the evil slickness of a German staff car emerging out of the shaded drive to park in front of the tall entrance doors. So over-powering were my feelings as I stood beside the bell pull, that I wondered where prosaic cabbages could possibly be hidden in this stately residue of the old regime. The cabbages had to be somewhere I knew, for I had seen cheerful posters in Paris advertising the Spring Perennial Festival and the Autumn Rose, Fruit and Vegetable Festival at Château St Jean de Beauregarde.

Built in the seventeenth century, the château was purchased in 1878 by the family of the present owner, Vicomte Bernard de Curel, changing little until it was requisitioned for occupation by German troops in 1940. When Muriel de Curel became chatelaine in the 1980s

rows of old fruit trees survived in the weed-choked potager, hidden behind high stone walls at the end of a path opposite the entrance to the house.

Using seventeenth-century plans still lodged in the château archives, Madame de Curel decided to remake the grand, 2 hectare (5 acre) potager. Following the classic potager design of a four-square grid cut by two main axes, the original garden fell into four quarters. The quarters were again subdivided into four beds, making sixteen beds in all. Today these beds are surrounded by softly grassed paths and outlined by flowers, extraordinary banks of annuals that form two crosses of lime, yellow and orange flowers, a cross of ethereal blue and another of sugar pinks.

The main axis of the garden continues to belong to the original espaliered trees, whose thick, nobly trunks coneal the clue to their true age. Many are still vigorous, holding erect hearty pear and apple branches espaliered into upright forks or the long, horizontal branches, or cords, that give testimony to the skills of long forgotten garden-ers. Replacement trees include 'Durondeau', a pear that was not yet in fruit, and a label on a green apple said 'Belle de Boskoop'. These two trees are part of the constant work of renewal carried out by Madame de Curel and a single gardener.

I first saw this epitome of the French potager as my watch said 6 am on a day that promised heat. Dew streaked the ripening, purple plums on the old, propped-up trees that lined the grass path from the potager gates, remnant from a time when many gardeners laboured to feed all the inhabitants of this domain.

Against the north wall of the garden herbaceous plants were subdivided by buttresses of green box. A collection of shade-tolerant plants – grey-leafed hostas, the mauve hoods of foxgloves, the dark acanthus, its huge leaves like

oval serrated platters, and *Pulmonaria officinalis*, with whitewash splashed leaves – spread out either side of the deep well in the stone wall. The large clumps of hardy day-lilies obviously loved this border, for they were repeated again and again, as were early-flowering peonies and *Aruncus dioicus*. At one point a climbing Hydrangea *petiolaris* created a mass of white flowers to clothe the wall, along with a sweet smelling honeysuckle.

On the sunny south wall opposite the vibrant red pear 'William Rouge' was espaliered among decorative grape vines, already giving a suggestion of crimson, and both were underplanted with sun-loving perennials. The west wall was banked with currant bushes, punctuated by vibrant pink dahlias. A broken wall on the eastern perimeter was smothered with old roses. Here I found the beautiful, papery-white blooms of *Rosa* 'Blanche Double de Coubert' among many rugosas, the lavender-grey leaves of the moss rose R. 'William Lobb' and the quartered teacups of the pale pink Bourbon rose *R.* 'Souvenir de la Malmaison'.

Parallel beds planted with cutting flowers were stopped by glasshouses festooned with grapevines. Now, as in monastic times, the enclosed vegetable garden gave way to meadow and orchard, a soft and serene sight so calming after the power of the intensely productive garden.

These *potagers fleuries*, or flowered vegetable gardens, are strictly rotated. One bed in each section is put down to green manure each year, planted with peas or lucerne to feed the soil. In the remaining three beds all the herbs and vegetables that the table craves are carefully planted in lines: artichokes, red chard, carrots, beans, leeks, lettuce, garlic, celery, cabbage, curly kale and fennel. Whole plots are devoted to berries, others to asparagus, pumpkins and potatoes, with an enormous corner occupied by cardoons.

It is not the immaculate rows or wide plots of abundant vegetables that dominate this garden, but the engulfing borders. These are huge, wide bands of massed annuals in tones of limey-yellow to gold or lavender blues and candy-striped pink and white, graded in height from giant dahlias to the small humps of furry ageratum, using every extreme of texture from the coarse, wide leaves of hairy sunflowers or *Nicotiana sylvestris*, to ferny Queen Ann's lace and velvet *Amaranthus hypochondriacus*. The plants are packed tightly together, as though corralling the more plebeian vegetables behind their incredible beauty. These are in truth 'display' gardens in the eighteenth-century manner.

There are a few days in every summer when an annual border reaches unsurpassed perfection, and I arrived at

Opposite left: Citrus colours glow in the yellow annual border adjacent to a resting bed sown to green manure, often with crops of peas or lucerne.

Opposite top right: *Nicotiana sylvestris*' long, white bells are offset by large lime leaves.

Opposite bottom right: A garden of artichokes planted in strict lines – it is hard to imagine that so much growth is required to harvest those small, delicious artichoke bottoms.

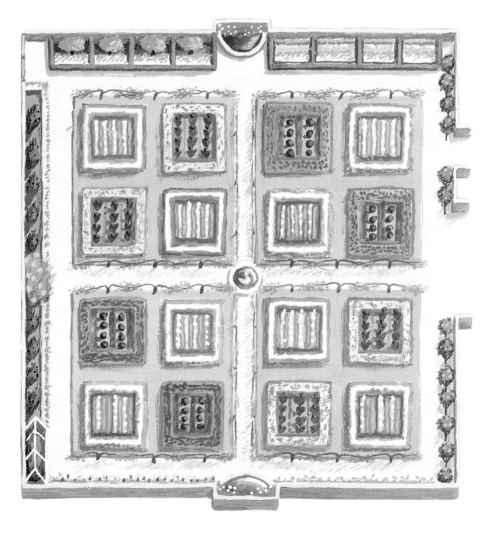

St Jean on the penultimate day. In the citrus border *Antirrhinum* in white and yellow, giant golden sunflowers, rudbeckia in deep gold, African marigolds, *Moluccella laevis*, the green bells of Ireland, tall stiff stems studded with pale green calyces. The tall *Nicotiana sylvestris* with wide lime leaves and slim white flowers, eye-high, feathery white cosmos and the powdery grey-white *Salvia farinacea*. Long green pendent tassels of *Amaranthus caudatus* and stiff bread-and-butter plates of a soft apricot dahlia echoed the daisy shapes through the beds. The planting combinations were repeated over and over again to enforce the desired effect.

Each border seemed even more breathtaking than the last. I fell totally for an ethereal mixture of the blue and white Salvia farinacea, stiff lilac-coloured zinnias and the white stars of the *Nicotiana alata*, alongside the taller *N. sylvestris*. The humble petunia in lavender blue lay before deep purple malvas, tall and bushy, with stiff-armed *Verbena bonarensis*. More lacy cosmos, the compact froth of lavender-coloured ageratum below dahlias, both large, icy white ones and soft pompoms of mauve. Like the vegetables, the flowerbeds are planted for annual enjoyment, soon to peak with the bounty of the garden.

At the crossing of the paths stood a classic urn filled with flowers. In the pink and white cross, the urn held pink and white geranium, anthirrhinum, petunia and, again, the grey and white Salvia farinacea, always tolerant of dry spaces.

Madame de Curel has a great interest in the historic context of the garden. In the vegetable patches there are old-fashioned varieties. Each year table grapes are preserved by the Thomery System. This takes place in a small store room where there are racks and racks of matching glass bottles, each filled with the purest spring water and a single bunch of grapes. In the *frutierer*, the fruit is arranged on four sloping wooden shelves. Nearby, an immense stone dovecote stands empty. Inside, the central pole still suspended, with two long ladders attached. These were used to harvest the doves, the battery chickens of a world without refrigerators.

The bones of this garden are old, steeped in the tradition of France. It is a vibrant *jardin potager*, that has the special quality of a garden that is the passion of one person. In this case, the person is both disciplined enough to achieve perfection and unrestrained by over-zealous authorities. St Jean de Beauregarde is a brilliant display of plant selection and colour sense, flowers, vegetables and herbs, climaxing in annual borders which are the inspired confections of an exceptional gardener.

Opposite: A bravura combination of the simplest plants and vegetables, verbena, *Nicotiana Sylvestris*, cosmos, Queen Ann's lace, cleome and red-veined chard seen here in front of long-leafed corn.

Below: In a garden famed for its unusual and historic vegetables, a group of burgundy amaranthus look like exotic fingers beside white antirrhinums and star-like nicotiana.

A fine veil of mist enshrouded the woods and fields. It was caught in the folds of hills, coating a village so it appeared only as a ghostly outline beside the road. Then the shroud quietly parted, revealing walls of tall hedges framing a large, symmetrical eighteenth-century château, its drive closed to the world by iron gates overhung by a single swag of roses.

I had come to Belgium to find one of Europe's most celebrated potagers, redesigned and planted in the latter part of the twentieth century by the late Countess Michael d'Ursel, whose love of gardening made this fine old garden a 'must see' for anyone who delights in the potager style.

On this grey, late summer afternoon, I looked down from the terrace and the potager unrolled like a ghostly carpet. A church spire hung as an eerie presence above, and long lines of perfectly tilled plants were starting to don the colours of autumn, casting a burnished glow. Lit now and then by flashes of regal colour, they acted as a reminder that this garden was conceived by Charles-Francois de Velbruck, an enlightened Prince and Bishop of Leige, who laid out 5 hectares (12 acres) of formal garden, surrounding it with a park inspired by the English landscape style of the eighteenth century.

All day the mists ebbed and flowed, finally lifting to reveal the most extraordinary line of dahlias in full flower, a bristling miscellany of colour. There was every possible style, with the cactus, pompom, and water lily types particularly well represented. It was an exuberant planting, monumental in conception.

The dahlias marched down either side of the great garden, holding it in check and imprisoning the massed rows of vegetables, herbs and cutting flowers. In this giant parade of jewelled colour, immense and immaculately staked plants created the most dazzling architectural edging behind precision-cut box hedges.

The entire garden was enclosed by walls that dripped with the colours of ripening fruit. There were seventeen different varieties of golden and russet-brown pears, many of their names long forgotten. 'Pitmaston Duchess' and 'Clapps Favourite' were well represented, both responding well to pleaching and training over arches and long walls. Low fences of bright red apples, polished by raindrops, included deep red 'Jonathan', the excellent cooking apple 'Belle de Boskoop' and 'James Grieve', which has the sweet, fresh taste of an apple just plucked from the tree. These international varieties grew among old and European varieties in the potager and orchard.

Apples and pears are perhaps the easiest trees to espalier. They look lush and vigorous as knee high, step-over fences, pruned so that the tree's strength is focused on the two single, outstretched branches forming the cord or cordon. Two branches are selected for training. They are bent from the main trunk on to the supporting wire, and then taped or tied in place. Unwanted branches are simply snipped

# KASTEEL HEX
## BELGIUM

Previous page: A fiesta of hot-coloured, summer annuals, zinnias and cosmos in the potager at Kasteel Hex.

Above: The wall of dahlias at Kasteel Hex.

off. If two parallel cordons are required, two branches are left to grow on either side of the trunk. The apple varieties selected for low fences are generally grafted on to dwarf root stock and spaced 2.5-3 m (8-10 ft) apart, while standard trees will train successfully on high walls. This is a slower process. The branches must be trained out as they grow, unless you cheat and buy a tree to train at the height you require. To keep the trees looking tidy, a simple summer pruning is necessary, with summer shoots cut back to reveal the desired shape.

Some of the trees in the garden date from the era of the Prince, 250 years ago. There are two ancient mulberry trees, curious medlar trees with their intriguing, brown fruit, and two varieties of fig: 'Brunswick', which enjoys the warmth of brick walls, and 'Brown Turkey', reliable here out of doors. Peaches, cherries, plums, raspberries, the ivory white currant 'White Versailles' and the translucent red currants 'Johkheer Van Tets' grew alongside the sweetest white strawberries.

The lines of the giant potager were long swatches of colour tightly bound in straight lines, their uneven texture firmly controlled to create the effect of a school girl's rag rug on a monster scale. There were lines of blue-grey onion tops (*Allium cepa*), silver-grey globe artichokes (*Cynara cardunclus*) and purple 'Red Orach', the red mountain or New Zealand spinach. Its red leaves made it look like a smouldering ember, cooling near curly parsley of the brightest green planted in wide bands.

The garden also produces potatoes and carrots and ten different brassicas. These were interspersed with an ever-increasing collection of culinary and aromatic herbs and bold cutting flowers. I saw long lines of lollypop-pink cosmos and a fiesta of bright zinnias growing among some of the fifty-two varieties of vegetables sown each year.

Unusual vegetable varieties, many of them Italian in origin, were introduced by the late Countess d'Ursel and are still specialities of the garden. A selection of chicories and endives along with edible flowers such as pansies, violets, calendulas and the golden trumpets of courgettes.

Roses have always been synonymous with Kasteel Hex.

Above: Autumn apples stored on straw, following centuries of tradition.

Above right: The brown fruit of the medlar, a small tree that deserves to be more widely grown.

Bottom right: Late season artichokes and dahlias lit by the firey-leafed orach.

The Prince left a rose garden where roses that are now centuries old still flower each season. The late Countess d'Ursel also had a passion for roses. She especially loved the lax, informal multi-floras, bred from Chinese roses brought to Europe in the nineteenth century, along with Damask, Gallica, Alba, and Musk roses that smother the walls and iron balustrade high above the potager.

Of great interest were the roses bred by Louis Lens, a noted Belgium rosarian, whose roses grow all over the garden. In the potager the Countess chose the shrimp-pink *Floribunda* 'Centenaire de Lourdes', one of the finest repeat-flowering roses that blooms until late autumn around the central pond.

At the first sign of frost, the autumn vegetables are lifted and transferred to the vegetable cellar. This delightful tradition protects cardoons, celery, turnips, carrots, parsnips, endive and chicory from frost and cold.

As at Villandry, the potager tends to overshadow any other gardens at Kasteel Hex. Even the astonishing

Chinese garden is outdone, despite an eighteenth-century pagoda sheltering a polychrome Buddha whose hands, head and tongue move with the wind. A regular, patterned, box-edged parterre is filled with perennials and there are formal lawns and terraces, with an ornamental park cut through by a majestic allée of plane trees.

Even when it is clothed in mist, the potager is obviously the pulsating heart of the garden. Loved and tended by descendants of the original family, it is one of Europe's most dramatic displays of vegetables, fruits, flowers and herbs. A masterpiece of simple, massed planting.

In place of the prettiness that we expect of the potager, Kasteel Hex offers us drama. It teaches us about the power of repetition in design. Line upon line is laid down in every imaginable colour, size and texture, and then a strong foil is employed as edging. Here it is the near colossal vulgarity of show-bench dahlias, the antithesis of the château, designed in the age of reason – a not to be missed lecture in the power of surprise.

Below right: Lush, curly parsley used as an edging plant.

Below: Late summer bounty hides behind large leaves.

Right: From the chateau terrace, the potager at Kasteel Hex.

Below: The potager is enclosed with apple draped walls, rose-coloured balustrades and miles of statuesque dahlias.

# CHAPTER 3
# OUTPOSTS

In the furthest outposts of an empire or on the frontiers of new worlds, gardens were made in fortified garrisons or behind high walls, sheltered enclaves in which plants could be protected from diverse marauders. The simple grid garden was adopted across the world as the neatest and easiest way to protect a precious source of food.

As the green woods, the jungle or the bush were tamed to meet European standards, a new and prosperous colonial society emerged. Its members soon abandoned their original settlements, leaving behind the first gardens they had made to emphasise the importance of their new position through the new, fashionable gardens that they then created. A few remaining trees, a briar rose entangled in a fence, the traces of an old building behind a modern facade, these are often the only clues of former habitation. Although they were abandoned, many of the old gardens were quietly remembered, and then simply remade within their original framework by a new generation, rediscovering the beauty of past designs.

# CHÂTEAU D'OPME
## FRANCE

A young priest stood in the hot sun, wearing a dusty soutane, a wide straw hat and impressively battered walking boots. He was surrounded by a gaggle of young people, all of them requesting entry to the château-fortress above.

The Château d'Opme has always stood on the pilgrim route along the narrow valleys of the Auvergne to Santiago di Compostella. Pilgrims, like the young priest that I saw, have always found a welcome at the twelfth-century, hill-top fortress.

The tightly packed small cars of eager garden visitors seem out of place in this setting, where iron-clad war horses would be a more suitable traffic, clattering along the cobbled street, past the huddled houses of the village. High above the fortified walls the brilliant red and yellow heraldic pennant of the Auvergne flutters.

The visitor enters the castle across a drawbridge leading into the first courtyard. This is a depressing, raked gravel square, overshadowed by looming black basalt walls, and I wonder why I have come. However, meeting the kindly owner quickly dispels my gloom, as we walk across a grassy terrace to the walled parapet and look down firstly on to an immaculate potager laid out within the battlements and then, with an eagle's-eye view, to the countryside stretching out far below.

The potager terrace is a large square divided into four sections around the central fountain. A brilliant green circle of grass centres each of these sections, a stunning effect against the patterns outlined in fire-red tufa gravel, which creates a theatre of colour beside the enclosing, black castle walls. The vegetable beds radiate out from the circles like opera fans. Well dug and manured, they are planted with familiar vegetables in all stages of growth, but inevitably the eye surreptitiously returns to those firm jets of water.

It is best to forget monastic tradition in this garden, for here, in this military stronghold, the water of life comes from the nipples of seventeenth-century naiads enfolded by the carved tendrils of the tree of life, an image certain to excite the imagination of any young novice.

This is not a large garden. It consists of a striking, geometric pattern, taken in at a glance as it hovers dramatically above the world. I felt like Jack in the Beanstalk, staring down at a miniature world of tiny towns and insect cars from a garden in the sky.

There are perfectly weeded rows of onions, their long leaves all carefully laid to one direction, their greyness echoed by the wide, blue leaves of cabbage. Alongside are bright green, low-growing, dwarf mangetout beans and white-stemmed chard. There are rows of multi-coloured lettuce in many styles, the taller growing cos, large butter lettuces, red and green oak-leafed varieties and decorative 'Lollo Rosso' accompanied by poles of ripening tomatoes and tightly staked dahlias, a multi-coloured parade adding a much needed gaiety to this garden eerie.

Espaliered apple trees were planted in 1993 along with the box edges to the main paths. To one side long beds of herbs grow haphazardly, tall red and pink hollyhocks tower in front of the steps that descend to the potager terrace and a rampant red rose is a vivid sight as it rambles over the black stone walls.

Created in 1991, this is a garden in the traditional French-château style, sited, as all good vegetable gardens were, at the lowest level, never pretending to be a grand *jardin potager* but a family garden, bringing a domestic peace to this formidable setting. However, it epitomises drama; the theatre of the black walls and the sharp red of the garden paths beside strong planes of green turf offer a lesson in hard landscape colour.

Opposite: From high on the battlements a bird's eye view of parterre and potager.

Left: The arresting, central fountain take pride of place in the potager.

Below: Cabbages and new sets of onions in the sky-high potager.

Following page: A garden still in its first decade has become a beautiful, traditional design in the manner of the best French potagers.

Below: Good husbandry, as after this crop of squash is harvested the compost will return to the garden.

Right: The house and garden that inspired the makers of some of America's finest estate gardens.

The fabled riches of the New World attracted Europe's adventurers. Others came to escape political and religious turmoil, determined to forge a new life.

Drawn from diverse countries, they left their architectural and horticultural thumb-prints in settlements across the continent: a flamboyant bougainvillaea over a Texan mission-house wall, lush courtyards in the deepest south and neat, clipped box hedges in front of Georgian brick and timber houses, from Maine to Savannah.

In the deep wooded hills that rise from the cool green waters of the Brandywine River, where native hostas grow in the dappled shade, what could be a French manor house stands on a bluff. It was built by Eleuthère du Pont Nimours, a French settler who wanted to pay tribute to the home he had left behind and laid out a *jardin potager* opposite his front door.

An ardent botanist, du Pont sent chests full of seeds to botanists and plant enthusiasts in Europe, so when he came to lay out his own garden he approached his family and friends. To his father he sent a plea for vegetable and flower seeds: 'You will realise how forlorn it is to live in the country and to have no garden, no fruit for the children.' du Pont asked his friend Louis Lelieur, Director of the gardens at St Cloud in France, to supply cherry, pear and plum trees. Lelieur responded to du Pont's request in 1802: 'It is a real pleasure to prove to you that you are right in counting on me to fill your garden with good things', he wrote, 'you will find the vegetable and flower seeds with the trees'. And so came 185 fruit trees, pears, apples, plum, cherry, sixteen grape vines, four nut trees, two black mulberry trees, three medlar trees and three 'peach apricot', packages of raspberries and roses, lavender and violas. Other requests went to France for the grape 'White Corinth', a rarity in America, as were grafted pears on quince to espalier as cones and cords.

Du Pont's grand-daughter Victoria drew a plan of the garden in 1880. It took the form of a quadrant that was three beds wide and four long, with at one end a semi-circular pond or 'turtle pen' overhung by a willow and enclosed by a hedge of lilac. There were tunnels of 'Chasselas', 'Muscat Blanc', 'Muscat violet' and 'Precox' grapes, and rustic French flowers were planted beside the vegetables. There was a parterre of roses with paths radiating from a central, round bed, but there were also cutting beds for roses and lines of currants, raspberries and gooseberries.

Louis Lelieur sent many roses from France, including 'Cent Feuilles', 'Rose des quatres saisons' and 'Rose pompone' to add to the locally grown 'Napoleon', 'Perpetuelle', 'Monsieur Rouge', 'Marie Louise', and 'Rose du Roi'. Du Pont, in his turn, searched America for plants. His gunpowder agents in Pittsburgh and New York supplied requests and his family sent seeds home from botanising trips in England, France, Spain, Portugal and Menorca.

The parterres were bordered by dwarf and espaliered peach and pear trees. Victoria recorded 'beds of strawberries and patches of melons', and there were also beds of

# DU PONT

# UNITED STATES

Above: These simple rows of flowers, vegetables and herbs could have been growing in any garden in rural France.

beets, carrots, turnips, parsnips, cabbage, broccoli, peas, beans, rhubarb, onions, gooseberry, raspberry and currant bushes, garlic, caraway, sweet marjoram, basil and summer savoury. A joyful mixture of flowers featured twenty-two different annuals, perennials and shrubs, including irises, lilies of the valley, camellias, mignonettes, nasturtiums, sweet peas and chrysanthemums.

Young Victoria du Pont, writing in 1822, recalls a walk during which she discovered scarlet columbines. 'I thought them so pretty', she said, 'that I brought home many with roots and planted them in our garden'. And so it was that European forest flowers and native American plants were admitted to an entirely French garden.

Victoria remembered that the paths were spread with yellow gravel and bordered by red bricks, but as the years went by neat box hedges with small corner cones replaced the espaliered edging. On the gentle slope above the garden stood an extensive orchard, from which cherries were harvested to make the childhood favourite 'cherry bounce' made from the . She also remembered how proud she was that their French chestnut trees were the first in America. *Papaver orientale* was grown in the garden 'from rare seeds sent from the Jardin des Plantes in Paris', where her father had studied, and these, too, were the first in the New World. Victoria also refers to a 'chestnut wind' at nut gathering time in October and humming birds flying above the old garden.

When Nick du Pont showed me around the garden, eighty-five years had passed since Victoria wrote her description. He walked with me through the woods beside the river, naming the native flowers and telling me about the old potager that he has worked so hard to restore. The garden was abandoned in the 1890s, but it was recorded in family letters and diaries, a garden plan and an exquisite watercolour. Today, lilac bushes still outline the 'turtle pen' and seven different varieties of espaliered apples decorate the perimeter of the garden, where originally twenty-one different pears and twenty-seven different apples grew.

Horizontal cords of the dwarf apples 'Golden Pearmaine', 'Starkey Delicious', 'Calville blanc d'Hiver', 'Esopus' and 'Spitzeinberg' stretch neatly along wires. Trained apples now cover the tunnel arbours and grafted pears, 'Bartlett' and 'Cornice', are shaped into tall cones.

Peter Lindner, the gardener, shakes his head sadly over the ravages of fire blight on the peach trees, where once forty-seven different varieties grew, and the raids of 'critters' on the newly planted seedlings. Nevertheless, the potager is becoming re-established in its historic river setting, with a summer vegetable crop as bountiful as ever it was.

The du Pont potager still retains the atmosphere of a

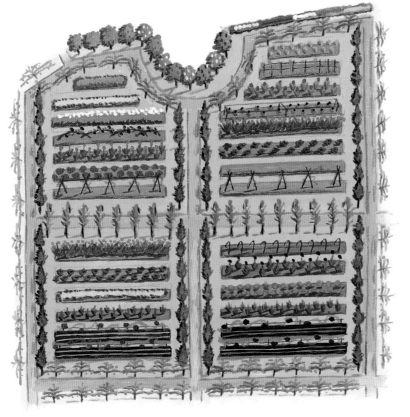

settler's vegetable plot dug in a clearing. The densely wooded hills that surround it preserve something of the atmosphere of unknown territory, ready to reclaiming the land if it is ever left untended.

Continuous planting ensures that carrots, parsnips, broccoli, onions, cabbage and cauliflowers ripen in a steady stream. The varieties, faithful to the old lists where possible, include 'Purple Cape' broccoli, cauliflower, dwarf peas and long, orange carrots. There are twenty-one types of vegetable in all, interspersed with dwarf marigolds, violas, coreopsis and stands of golden sunflowers, perhaps not quite so large as the forty-inch flowers that had delighted Victoria in the summer of 1823. The sculptured leaves of grey artichokes, ferny asparagus, wide-leafed rhubarb and feathery dill rise above tough skinned cantaloupes and nasturtiums, creating a summer display of Inca gold. Lima beans cling to tall poles, while small dwarf beans are immaculately tilled beside a long line of bright, spiky dahlias.

A glory of today's potager are the compost heaps, built in long lines approximately 1m (3ft) wide, stretching from path to path. They grow as the spent vegetables are added, sometimes reaching a height of 1.5m (5ft). Layer upon layer of leaves create stripes of different colours, making the heaps look like the best quality terrines. Left undisturbed for a year, the piles rot down to waist height, and at this point they become the most luxuriant beds for bright pumpkins, giving vertical height in the best *jardin potager* tradition. The long lines of giant green leaves make solid shapes among the finer lines of other vegetables. After use as a pumpkin bed for a single season, the compost returns to the garden as nutritious fertiliser.

A tall, white pump on wooden staging is a replica of the pump in the watercolour of 1873. Nearby, the rose parterre

has been brought back to life, with twenty fine varieties of old roses radiating from a central holly bush. Lavender bushes perfume the hot July day and culinary herbs are again part of the old design.

It could be said that this nineteenth-century du Pont garden was among the most influential in America. Its simple beauty inspired some of America's most famous gardens, for the second generation of du Ponts established the great estate gardens of Longwood, Winterthur and Nemours, that today attract thousands of visitors. While the old garden on the banks of the Brandywine River gently faded away, it was never forgotten. Reborn, it is once again a simple, abundant and fragrant garden steeped in the timeless French tradition.

Above: Long lines of compost are built like a terrine with layers and layers of vegetable leaves stacked neatly one upon another.

# ROSE BAY COTTAGE
## AUSTRALIA

The American War of Independence may have started with a ripple as tea was flung into Boston Harbour, but the ripples spread. The loss of the American colonies was humiliating for Mr Pitt's government, but it also caused a crisis in the British judicial system. America had been invaluable as the final destination for felons as endentured servants. Desperate to get shot of its 'criminal classes', the British Government remembered the strange land described by Captain Cook seventeen years earlier. Hastily assembled, an expedition of eleven ships left England and landed at Botany Bay. Moving on to Sydney Cove on the afternoon of January 26, 1788, they rowed ashore, claiming it in the name of George III and calling it Australia.

The specimens brought back by Sir Joseph Banks, Captain Cook's botanist on his voyage to the South Seas, had caused great excitement among the cognoscenti of London. However, the 1,030 people who sailed past the primeval landscape of Sydney Harbour felt more fearful than curious. They would have seen the tall, biscuit-coloured cliffs, and trees that looked like victims of acute dermatitis, their bark hanging from them in long strings. Beneath the trees were weird shrubs with sawn-edged leaves and cones which resembled the faces of trolls or gremlins. The colonists knew nothing of the soils, rainfalls or temperatures of the totally alien landscape, where they were expected to reconstruct the English way of life.

Starvation, isolation, rebellion and rum nearly destroyed the fledgling colony, but within forty years beautiful Georgian houses were gracing the harbour foreshores. One of the most charming of all was Rose Bay Cottage, designed by John Verge, the most fashionable colonial architect of his day. It overlooked a pristine bay about seven miles from Sydney Town. Well-tended gardens facing the foreshore contained the productive beds vital for colonial survival. They were far removed from the circular carriage drives, lawns and flowerbeds laid out in front of the new homes similar to those of prosperous English merchants in Liverpool, Manchester or Bristol, the inspiration behind many an idealised colonial garden.

The history of Rose Bay Cottage epitomises the colonial story. The land overlooking the bay was quickly acquired by the colony's most flamboyant entrepreneur, Captain John Piper H.M. Collector of Customs, who was highly successful as a society figure and as a financier until an 1826 audit of his accounts! Piper's bankrupt estate was bought by Daniel Cooper and Solomon Levy, two

Below: A rampant passion fruit vine decorates one of Sydney's oldest verandas.

ex-convicts who had amassed fortunes from trading in seals, wool and timber. Levy later returned to England to finance the settlement of Western Australia, while Cooper's young cousin, John Holt, came out to find work and eventually became a director of the Bank of New South Wales and a city councillor. So much for the Georgian social theory about clearing out the irredeemable criminal classes!

Today, much of the site of Rose Bay Cottage garden is covered by very desirable villas and apartments, jostling for harbour views, but the old house has been rescued and sympathetically restored. A much smaller garden has been planted, acknowledging the period of the house and the local flora. In a central, U-shaped court yard, a very 'Sydney' interpretation of a *jardin potager* has been set out. Here, the climate is nearly subtropical, making European vegetables and plants grow at an enormous pace, bolting away so quickly that the leaf vegetables grow almost too fast to be practical.

Like so many early Australian houses, Rose Bay Cottage has a low-hung veranda, breaking the symmetry of the Georgian facade. Facing the courtyard, it is swathed with sturdy, deep green passion fruit vine, laden by March with dull, armadillo-like, green and purple fruit that produces delicious seeds and pulp. Its verdant green complements the ochre walls of the house and the warm red brick paths that divide the courtyards. Bricks, always a good material for building paths, are synonymous with Sydney.

Bricks make ideal pavers. A potager garden needs regular attention and a full wheelbarrow must have a firm, even surface to trundle along. Heavy and often violent rain storms can wash gravel paths into nearby gutters, whereas brick drains quickly, ensuring that paths are passable.

From the well-prepared soil, rich in organic matter that

now covers the sandy coastal soil, tomatoes climb sturdy tripods on the outer rim of this small garden. Yates, Sydney's best-known and oldest seed merchant, recommends the large, smooth 'Grosse Lisse' as the tomato best suited to the coastal climate, which is humid, hot and often wet during the summer. 'Tiny Tim', a miniature tomato, will self-seed anywhere, and the oval 'Roma' is excellent for preserving and sauce making. All are virtually pest free and suited to the local climate.

Above: Clipped bay trees and wigwams of sweet-peas anchor this small potager, while a central patch of garlic creates modern sculpture.

Sweet peas enjoy the strong Sydney sunlight, reaching over 2m (6ft) on their tripods next to the tomatoes. Around the feet of each tripod is a skirt of lush silver beet, the local name for Swiss chard. 'Fordhook Giant' always produces exceptional results, with clean white stalks beneath wide, crinkly, paddle-shaped leaves of deep, dark green. Silver beet will bolt quickly in this climate, but can be kept in check by regular topping. The long, warm days of summer ensure that the coriander, or Chinese parsley, flowers early. It is a tall, fine plant, looking like a lighter version of Queen Anne's lace, but with the pungent taste and aromatic smell prominent in 'Pacific Rim' cuisine.

Large, dominant mounds of rhubarb claim a corner by the steps, happily tolerating sun or shade. Rhubarb is a staple of old Australian vegetable gardens, surviving with the minimum of fertiliser, water or fuss. Easily grown, it also featured regularly in older Australian cookbooks. Next to the rhubarb is an asparagus bed where the plants seem to appreciate the cool, shady site assigned to them.

The globes of white onions were already showing above the ground, their slim, grey-green, pointed foliage making a vertical statement. However, the stalks of the garlics made dramatic loops and 'S'-bends, like garden sculpture designed to enhance the overall picture.

Herbs and aromatic plants are smartly clipped and the glossy, narrow-leafed bay trees are cut into a topiary shape, creating a focal point and providing structural interest.

Basils, in several varieties, are planted in late spring. Clumps of light green, feathery dill and fennel, its near relative, grow near mint. Although mint can become a garden curse, its rhizomes spreading as an impenetrable mat, it is bliss to sit by a mint bed on a summer's night, where verities perfume the air with peppermint, spearmint, apple or eau-de-cologne. Citrus trees, lemons and oranges grow to one side of the herbs, and flowers and roses climb a neighbouring fence, adding their spice to this very aromatic garden.

A long, oval bed in the centre of the potager caught my attention immediately. It was rimmed with the polished, grey, stone-like leaves of the echeveria, clustered rosettes of silver grey making a permanent edge of reflected light. An imaginative colour contrast to the red path, it opened my eyes to another wonderful edging plant that will tolerate the parched conditions of beds made next to gravel or brick. It requires little attention and, preferring to be abandoned, it will grow in most temperate zones, if given adequate air and sunlight.

As I looked at this clear, grey ring of light, other plants that I had known during my childhood sprang to mind. Everyone had an aunt with an old pot or tin containing the swollen, succulent fingers of *Senecio repens* somewhere in her yard. *Sempervivum tectorum*, the house leek, was another favourite. It is a perfect, pink-topped rosette that handles difficult locations beautifully. Both plants will thrive in any garden that enjoys hot summers and porous soils, making an excellent, informal alternative to the clipped hedges that so often edge paths and beds. I like the thought of *Echeveria* 'Violet Queen', with its purple leaves and grey centres, rimming lavender beds or the rubbery, blue rosettes of *Echeveria secunda* var. *glauca* in front of a bed of mixed herbs, especially the fine, silver-grey curry plant whose aroma conjures up an Indian kitchen. Even if the garden is in the Mediterranean zone, the perfect climate for these plants, think twice if you have doves or pigeons in the neighbourhood. My birds had great sport decimating a large pot of the low growing, juicy succulent *Haworthia* 'Grey Ghost' on their way to breakfast on new lettuces and any other seedlings.

Below: Rosettes of echeveria make an unusual edging for a potager.

At Rose Bay, garden designer Michael Cook has not attempted a historic recreation, but has set out the favourite plants of an older Australia in the potager style. A little further along Sydney Harbour is historic Vaucluse House, where a faithful re-creation of an early Australian kitchen garden, with its straight lines of vegetables and fruit trees, is attracting enormous attention. But Rose Bay Cottage unaffectedly adopts a continental potager style, combining traditional plantings with often overlooked succulents so suitable for a warm climate garden.

Below: *Echeveria secunda* var. *glauca*

'Gold!' read the headline of the Melbourne Argus in 1851, and within the year a stampede of 30,000 people streamed into this very small valley. They came from every part of the globe to pan for gold, for this was the richest alluvial gold field in the world. Over time they transformed the pristine bushland, giving it:

*...the dismal appearance of a graveyard, men washing dirt in tubs, carrying its colour on their skin, hair, hat, trousers and books, miserable looking low tents their places of refuge. Where water was to be seen it was a puddle. The whole scene was one of unspeakable squalor. The firing of guns, pistols and revolvers made the night hideous – robbery with violence being frequent. Our tent was cut open twice, but the cocking of our revolvers being heard warned the intruders off.*
RECORDS OF THE CASTLEMAINE PIONEERS

Today, Forest Creek is a sleepy backwater an hour's drive from Melbourne. The humps and bumps of old diggings bear testimony to those turbulent years, as do occasional clumps of tall poplars or pines, gnarled apple trees and tangles of willows. These are peaceful reminders of the glory days, when the trees were probably planted by a homesick miner in front of his cottage. Now a narrow country road passes Poverty and Dead Man's Gully, eerily evocative names, before crossing the creek into Golden Gully, where a tiny miner's cottage looks out over the clear water.

Thickets of European trees stand in the shelter of a hill covered in eucalypts and wattle, where a path through the rough grass leads to a dry stone wall, now nearly hidden by the rampant roses that enclose a carefully designed potager. The main axis of the oblong garden is a path

# THE POTAGER NEAR CASTLEMAINE
## AUSTRALIA

Above: giant artichokes spill over the rock edges, relishing the hot, dry summers of Victoria

Right: surrounded by natural grey bush, the potager looks at peace with its surroundings

Following page: in summer, herbs colonise every rock crevice, casting a blue-grey pall over the garden

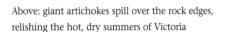

that crosses the plot at an angle, arriving at a round, gravel centre point before continuing its way up two levels to a gate at the far side. The curved beds which radiate from the central circle are cut by dissecting paths. Each bed is raised by nearly 60cm (2ft) and encased in rock walls of the local bluey-grey stone. They are beautiful to look at, but the walls turn the beds into miniature ovens in the summer and, to compensate, the plants are mulched with a thick covering of straw, which protects their roots and retains all available moisture.

This garden was no chance creation. It is tended by a well-known food specialist who brought culinary sophistication to this secluded backwater. The sun-loving *Rosmarinus officinalis* 'Prostratus', a native of the Mediterranean, thrives in the rock pockets , its small, wiry leaves trailing over the rock face. All types of thyme and prostrate perennials cling to the stone. I spied the pink-flowered lemon thyme, *T. citriodorus*, spreading to make a thick bank that was reminiscent of the 'bank whereon the wild thyme blows' in *A Midsummer-Night's Dream*. Many thymes had self-seeded into odd crevices. *Thymus vulgaris*, the evergreen French thyme with its aromatic leaves and pale lavender flowers, along with the bees that always hover close by, and silver posy thyme. Sages, silver, grey and purple, loved this well-drained, sunny position. Blanketed with flowers during summer, this is one of the easiest herbs to grow, as it tolerates both snow and heat.

The lavenders, *Lavandula angustifolia*, *L. dentata* and *L. stoechas* tumbled on to paths, down walls and over flowerbeds, their oils warm on the surface of the leaves.

The deep blue *Borago officinalis* – a family friend of comfrey – is grown today for its never-ending, blue, summer flowers. Here it has overtaken some of the beds

and self-seeded between gravel and rocks. Small mounds of marjoram are to be seen, together with its close relative oregano. They are similar in appearance, but marjoram has small grey-green leaves, whilst those of the oregano are a lighter green. Both are essential herbs in Mediterranean cooking. The stronger flavour of oregano comes through in pasta sauces, moussaka and pizza, whilst the more delicate marjoram is ideal with chicken, fish and vegetables. Together with thyme and sage it is part of the traditional trilogy of mixed herbs.

Groups of chives with their mauve pompoms add to the mauve-blue aura of this garden. Chives should be divided regularly to keep the clumps looking fresh. They are very easy to grow, even in the poorest soil, but they can become straggly and bushy if not harvested regularly in summer. I have read that chives help defy powdery mildew on cucumbers, so this season in they will go around my cucumbers, which always seem to have diseased leaves. Garlic chives have wider leaves and white flowers; growing to 60cm (2ft). They have a stronger taste and can be used as an alternative edging plant. At the other end of the spectrum is *Allium sativum*, garlic, whose tall stalks grow from multiple rice-paper-wrapped cloves of pungent flavour, ready to harvest six months after planting. By this time the plant looks dreadful, brown and shrivelled and could be accused of spoiling the look of the potager, but it is a vital ingredient in European and Asian food and hardy in most climates.

Many of the vegetables in this garden were grown from Bulleri seeds imported from Salerno in Italy. Bulleri initially supplied Melbourne's large European-migrant communities, but other gardeners have now seized upon their seeds. Among their basil seeds was 'Toscano a foglia di lattuga', a giant basil with lettuce-sized leaves. There are nineteen different types of chicory, ranging from the very long, thin, green and white striped leaves of 'Catalogna del Veneto' to a round, cabbage-like chicory called 'Variegata di Castelfranco' with a heart that looks as if a vermilion paint brush has been cleaned all over it. There are also seven types of endives and 'Carciofo grosso romanesco', an artichoke with a perfectly round ball of green-purple, and the adventurous, long-leaved 'Cardo Gigante di Nizza, that translates as 'large thistle from Nice,' but is in fact an unusual chard. Soon to be planted in the potager were several of Bulleri's varieties of tomatoes and peppers. I am going to try their prettiest aubergine, it is the palest lavender 'Melanzana bianca stumata di rosa'.

The greatest joy I have when visiting gardens is finding new varieties of plants. Gardeners are the friendliest of people. They will find an old packet of seed for you under piles of tackle in the potting shed, or lend you a seed catalogue. This is how I learnt that these excellent Italian varieties are now available in Australia.

The gardener of the potager near Castlemaine had enclosed the site with a thicket of espaliered apple trees and mountainous roses. Although this is a grid layout in the formal style, the garden has been allowed to paint its own pictures. Its curving stone beds are at one with the old landscape; shades of lavender blue dominated the herb beds that hot summer afternoon, complementing to the blue-grey of the surrounding bushland. It harmonised so well it looked less like a foreign invasion than the accepted vegetable patch.

Opposite: the grey of *Stachys byzantina*, teucrium and artichoke harmonise with the thymes and roses

# CHAPTER 4
# TRADITIONAL
# INTERPRETATIONS

The gardens in this section of the book were scattered over three continents. Their gardeners came from a variety of cultural backgrounds, and yet a common theme ran through them all, as their creators drew inspiration from the accepted wisdom of the past. Perhaps this is why I found these gardens so intriguing. For I was fascinated to see the unique interpretation of the traditional potager style made by each gardener.

Three of these traditional potagers were made by some of England's most talented designers, where their structural details owed more to the ideals of the nineteenth century than the twenty-first. Their beauty is oblivious to new trends, such as the contemporary potager that displays its plants as the outline of the human genus.

Although the layout of these gardens was traditional, their rich diversity of plant material was entirely contemporary. Their creators promoted gardening for colour and design as well as for the simple pleasure of growing their own plants. They worked to create garden pictures from varied flowers, leaves and stems, lifting the conventional style to new realms through colourful experimentation.

It was the perfect English picture: a Regency, stone rectory screened from the twisting village street by carefully chosen shrubs. The windows of the drawing room opening on to a sweeping lawn bordered by summer perennials. However, in the walled garden, where rows of well-tilled vegetables and occasional fruit tree of the English kitchen garden should have grown, there was a sudden change. Instead of the predictable vegetable garden there was a perfect French potager, screened by high walls from the quintessentially English picture beyond. A cruciform grid divided the potager into four. It was subdivided again into further grids of four by very small, square beds bordered by box, then outlined once more by long, narrow plots.

The Old Rectory garden is a very twentieth-century adaptation of the potager style, a pleasing configuration of beautiful features in an idyllic setting. Tall apple arches cross the main path and the centre of the garden is marked by diagonal arches, draped in early summer by cascades of creamy-white *Rosa* 'Félicité Perpétue', a familiar potager choice. The arches span practical but decoratively detailed brick and stone paths.

The garden was designed by Rosemary Verey, and it has much in common with her other potager gardens. A network of narrow paths divided the minute beds, but the planting choices were bold, the plants often oversized. Dominant, vertically trained climbers gave strength to a design that might otherwise have been almost too pretty and orderly.

When I visited the Old Rectory, the huge, creeping, Cinderella-coach pumpkin, 'Rouge d'Etampes', was almost ripe, bringing to mind the pumpkin faces of Halloween. The garden's unusual range and variety of plants are drawn from American, French and English vegetable seed catalogues. This is the work of Annie Huntington, the

American-born owner of the garden, who masterminds the splendid combinations of plant colour and texture.

Red was a dominant colour in the late-summer garden. It was captured in the 'Bulls Blood' beetroot, generally grown just for its intensely coloured leaves. A few of the ruby-veined leaves torn up create high drama in a bowl of mixed greens. Beside the beetroot, carrots grew in clumps. There was a hint of orange as the maturer roots pushed up through the soil beside the red, speckled oak-leaf lettuce 'Fortune' that carried through the colour story.

In another bed 'Strawberry', a diminutive, American, red popcorn, was planted near to the raspberries-and-cream 'Pink Perder' strawberry, surrounded by variegated leaves. The ruby-red kernels of the popcorn are miniature red hot pokers surrounded by dry, silvered cream husks, that can bring a glow of autumn colour to a mid-winter house that will last until the following summer.

Nearby, the purply-red leaves of red orach, the wild spinach that was already over 1m (3ft) tall, had been allowed to push through tripods of pink 'Painted Lady' sweet pea, which were interwoven with groups of giant, purple *Allium giganteum* and bronze Florence fennel. Elsewhere, 'Lemon Queen' the sunflower that takes its colours from the Van Gogh painting, grew alongside small, mature pompoms of chives at ground level and regal, red, climbing 'Empress of India' nasturtiums which fought a scarlet 'Roma' tomato for space on elegant, silvered, spiral frames from France.

Opposite: Soft pink sweetpea 'Painted Lady' against the moody, red-purple leaves of Red Orach, both jostling to see who will be the tallest.

Left: Ornamental kale Northern Lights 'Rose'.

Below: Tiny beds tightly planted with onions, lettuce and beans.

Following page: Standards of David Austin's English rose 'Heritage' capture the elegance of this Rosemary Verey designed garden.

# THE OLD RECTORY

# UNITED KINGDOM

Right: Chives line up to add cheerfulness and colour.

Below right: Giant kales rival the standard rose 'Heritage' at summer's end, and will make excellent eating during the darkest days.

Below left: The darkest purple leaves of Brussels sprout 'Rubine'.

Following page: Lines of golden oregano are part of the lettuce pattern of new green 'All The Year Around' and bronze 'Lumina'.

Box hedges planted around the smaller beds had been allowed to grow knee high, leaving only enough room for a very few plants in each bed. Wide-leafed, giant kales made a mockery of their tiny, hedged bed, straining to escape their confinement. 'Red Russian,' with red-veined leaves on purple stems, is a neon strip to light up the garden as the mercury falls, and the dark, underwater, blue-green 'Lacinato' is so primeval in appearance that it has been called 'the dinosaur kale'. Kale is an excellent winter meal, chopped, steamed and sautéed with butter, it complements the potatoes, smoked meats and sausages of winter fare.

In the long arbour there were kiwi fruits, their bright green flesh wrapped in rough, brown, army great coats, as well as eccentrically-shaped gourds and the summer squash 'Cocozelle', with its long, slender, dark green

pin-stripes. This hung beside a deep yellow courgette called 'Gold Rush Verity'. Smooth and cylindrical, this American variety of courgette is the richest and most golden of colours. Clematis and Muscat grapes were desperately trying to stake their claim in this darkening tunnel of climbers.

On either side of the entrance, espaliered peaches were protected by a glass sheet that served both to protect the 'Duke of York' peach from the curly leaf spores that are carried with the rain and reflect warm air on to the ripening fruit. Apricots, pears and nectarines also benefited from the warmth of the red brick walls, along with *Rhodochiton atrosanguineus*, a compact vine covered with double, bell-shaped caps of a dusty purple, like bells from a Chinese temple.

Bright, polished, red apples were trained as cords along low, wooden fences, so perfect and colourful that they seemed to belong to a varnished painting. They were underplanted with green or white variegated strawberry leaves and the 'Munsted' lavender. Other apples had been trained into lollipop sentinels. The English, blush-pink rose 'Heritage' was growing beautifully. I have found it to be one of David Austin's most successful varieties. Given constant feeding and daily water in summer, it becomes one of the best garden roses.

Tall wigwams completely filled many of the neat, square beds. They were covered with *Tomatillo physalis ixocapa* 'Roma Verde', a clinging, prolific vine with translucent, papery pods in shades of faded orange and pale rust, along with the petite, light green globes of 'Rondo de Nice' courgettes, tangled with mint-green, cylindrical 'Clarimore', a courgette with a creamy texture and exceptional flavour.

As mid-summer sweet peas faded, their wigwam was claimed by the passion-flower vine *Passiflora incarnata*,

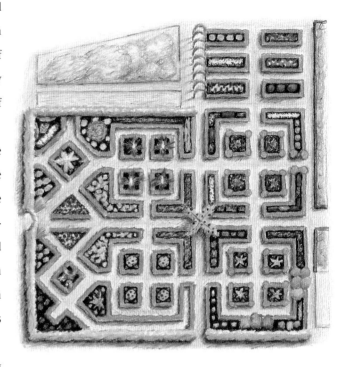

with its whorls of white and purple petals. This is a plant that can only be bedded out when the earth is warm. Mexican cathedral bells, *Cobaea scandens*, created cups and saucers of velvety blue and lavender flowers and gave off a honeyed perfume. Another of my favourites from this American selection was the standard, deep purple heliotrope 'Chatsworth'. Planted in terracotta pots, it made bold colour points above a paler heliotrope, 'Princess Marina,' used as smaller plants to create contrast.

This is an exceptionally pretty and productive garden with a wide selection of plants. Along with all the vegetables I have described, there are also dozens of varieties of beans and lettuces, as well as tomatoes that grow in every shape, colour and texture. The overall effect of this beautiful twentieth-century design with pocket-sized beds is that of a canvas for an ever-changing picture of unusual plants, where an enquiring gardener has enjoyed the thrill of experimentation.

The valley of the Whitewater, only 80 kilometres (50 miles) from London, was a favoured valley in the Middle Ages. The river flowed past a royal hunting lodge and a castle in Odiham Forest, before meandering gently through fields, past water mills and on to loop behind an old farmhouse at West Green.

Historical evidence suggests that the pond at West Green predates the Elizabethan manor, a building that was drastically rearranged by General Hawley when he built West Green House in 1720, leading historians to argue that there has been a productive garden at West Green House for many centuries.

Today's garden lies within walls erected by General Hawley in around 1770. The remains of old hedges and apple trees show that the garden has for many years been divided in two, and still one half is devoted to herbaceous borders, while the other is divided again into two squares centred on a graceful, hexagonal fruit cage.

When I arrived at West Green House, the vegetable garden had been abandoned for some years, the wonderful cages so frail that when we touched them they collapsed. Large in scale, the squares and paths were outlined with a few remaining box plants that were old and scraggy and desperate for pruning and nourishment. Two years of clearing and rebuilding followed, leaving a spacious canvas on which we could totally redesign the vegetable garden.

As my fruit and vegetable requirements were minimal, I decided to make this an entirely fanciful garden, for the adjoining herbaceous borders were being restocked with only the most acceptable plants, and I was fearful the whole garden could slip into polite boredom unless these plots were imaginative and fun.

I laid the greater part of the ground down to herbs. Santolina was planted in three large groups and clipped as balls. Two more plots were filled by ever-decreasing and descending squares of lavender, finishing with a stoechas variety, a low-growing cultivar which we kept clipped as tiny hedges, trimming them twice a year. The bracts of this lavender are purple-blue with pointed, bumble bee wings on top. The *L. stoechas* subsp. *pedunculata* detested the wet winter last year, as did the burgundy *L. stoechas* subsp. 'Helmsdale'. However, quickly replanted in early spring, they were forming hedges by the autumn.

Initially, I covered large stretches of ground with different varieties of thyme. This proved more labour intensive than regularly hoeing vegetable beds, for fine thyme and fine weeds are like entwined lovers, impossible to disentangle without the loss of both. Sage proved to be the better proposition, growing to knee height in mounds. The dense, oval, grey-green *Salvia officinalis* smothered weeds and formed attractive, rounded shapes. I am told that there are over 700 varieties of sage, but I found *Salvia officinalis purpurea*, its grey leaves backed by deep purple, *S. officinalis* 'Icterina', a brilliant, golden sage, and S. officinalis

# WEST GREEN HOUSE
## UNITED KINGDOM

Above: Burgundy kale just about to push through
and tower above the sweetpeas, *Cerinthe major*
'Purpurascens' and Red Drumhead cabbages.

Opposite: The ornamental kale 'Kamome white'.

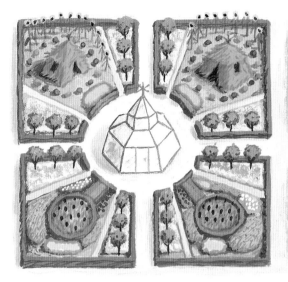
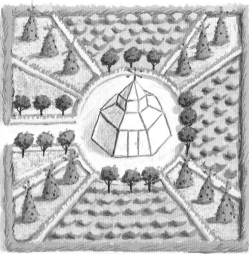

'Tricolour', white, pink and green, combined beautifully to make two large, fragrant mats.

Nearby, I planted my 'Red Drumhead' cabbages, again in decreasing squares, with lines of *Cerinthe major* 'Purpurascens' and a tall, curly 'Tuscan Black' kale, believing that the sage would repel cabbage moths from this sea of blue, purple and grey. I don't think it helped at all, but it is a pleasing colour combination and one to be repeated again.

Rue can be trimmed and closely planted as small balls in massed patterns, that could, I believe, rival santolina to create clipped sculpture. It too is said to repel insects, or even the plague, and it was an important ingredient in witches' brews. So, all in all, it has all the characteristics needed to grow in my garden.

Each season, I separate the three blocks of santolina balls with four long wedges of vegetables and flowers, tall wig-wams of sweet peas or beans. Strands of coloured corn or sunflowers form a backbone, with plants of decreasing height filling every patch of earth by the autumn's end.

Amaranthus is a strange and wonderful plant, grown for thousands of years by the American Indians as a cereal crop. I grow it for its weird and challenging shapes. *Amaranthus giganticus*, the 'elephant's head' amaranthus, has enormous, deep purple protuberances, like an appalling case of elphan-tiasis, while *Amaranthus hypochondriacus* 'Burgundy' has arms like those of a furry tarantula spider. Hardy, drought-tolerant plants, they bring an air of mystery to any garden.

The tall, dark castor oil plant (*Ricinus communis*) is another giant to replace beans and peas towards summer's end, its deeply cut leaves and coral-red flowers contrast with the colour of the amaranthus.

One year I arranged woven hurdles in a diamond shape and filled them to the brim with rich compost before planting each bed in early spring with potatoes, then

Below: The orange-gold sweetpea 'Air Warden' and sunflowers with an orange tripod; late summer sun lights the leaves of the bolting lettuce 'Cerise'.

Opposite: Santolina balls and lavender hedges.

replanting with those knuckle dusters of the garden world, rampant gourds and marrows in shades of topaz and gold, especially the stripe-topped 'Turks Turban' and 'Crown of Thorns'. The result was reminiscent an illuminated manuscript and the contained site proved ideal for these unruly vegetables.

Last year fantasy carried us even further when these two patches became the gardens for Hansel and Gretel cottages, the planting a tribute to the cottage gardens of middle Europe. The buildings were made from garden stakes, with climbing beans of different colours, carefully tied to form doors and windows around blue and red painted frames. The whole project caused much laughter. My good friend and gardener Mike Rendell became an architect and builder, and his son Dominic, the Head Gardener, became the painter. David Chase, who is a plantsman extraordi-naire, decided that the cottage gardens must have paths. As a result, curved paths appeared in the beds and we four adults had the best fun planting the gardens, indulging the childish fantasies that remain with us all.

The walls of the bean cottage were covered with tried and tested varieties such as 'Purple Giant'. This vigorous, deep purple bean made the side walls, while 'Scarlet Runner' provided the roof. The red and white splashed Borlotto 'Tongues of Fire' filled in around windows and doors.

I decided that the front gardens of the cottages should be a tri-coloured cauliflower patch, orange 'Marmalade', bright green 'Emerald' and deep purple 'Violet Queen', with the miniature, white cauliflower 'Idol' to line the edges. It would have looked delightful if the wood pigeons had not taken a fancy to them too, so hastily the tiny petunia 'Tasting Red' quietly draped itself over the decimated leaves. The deeply-cut leaves and red tops of the radish 'Scarlet Globe' were colour spots beside the path, along

with French marigolds, the summer mainstay of so many flowering vegetable gardens. Our garden centre yielded up 'Petite Mixed', which has bright yellow centres on ruffs of gold, yellow and orange.

We framed the house with single hollyhocks and erected a backyard of very tall sunflowers called 'Golden Giant', with the daisy form flower of Rudbeckia 'Goldilocks' at their feet to repeat the single flower shape. Scampering nasturtiums tried to cover the whole effect, but had not succeeded by the time I had to leave England.

This garden proved to be fun, colourful and productive, giving joy to its creators and to many who saw it. I view gardens as enchanted places. I like to grow plants so tall that I feel like the dormouse hidden by flowers. I also see the garden as somewhere to saturate myself in scents and tingle to the feel of satin or velvet petals. I like to taste peas from the vine and rub fresh mint leaves on my hands. A potager allows me to indulge all my senses and emotions at the same time.

The potager tradition invites experimentation with plants and designs. As I write, the blue cabbages are becom-ing a river, tall cosmos, and corn become riverside rushes beside cardoons that could be mistaken for a ghost-like forest, where the spirit of an American brave might canoe down our cabbage river, his cargo the medicinal plants that, along with other plants mainly from the Americas, provide an alternative interpretation of the *jardin potager*.

In another part of the potager we are looking to the Jacobean gardening tradition for our inspiration. Whatever I do, this garden will always be a combination of vegetables, fruit, flowers and herbs, grown together to give pleasure to the senses, while using plants from many nations to provide hours of enjoyment in planing and planting and to give great scope to a rampant imagination.

# HASELEY COURT
## UNITED KINGDOM

It is very hard to write about true love – a springtime affair can be guiltily analysed and endlessly discussed, but then put aside as no more than an enjoyable experience. I have affairs with gardens every season. Last summer it was the great blocks of grasses in an American garden, the year before a plum-tree maze that was to swoon for. One's true love, however, is more difficult to analyse. It has so many facets of beauty, wit and indefinable style.

My dream garden is Haseley Court in rural Oxfordshire. In truth, it consists of three very separate gardens, remote from each other in style, and each made to act out a different part. Two are green gardens, ingenious designs needing just one set of tones to create their special theatre.

The first garden, which reaches out from a handsome stone house, is a giant, sunken chess board. Set out with sixteen chessmen clipped from English box and four castles clipped from 2.5m (8ft) high yews are mighty green giants waiting eternally for the next move.

In deep shade, a garden to the rear of the house leads to a dark green stretch of water crossed by a carved stone bridge. The water is channelled to descend into a wilderness of native trees.

The walled garden is divided, in time honoured style, into four quarters by two crossed paths lined with old roses. There are those velvety-puce ones, *Rosa* 'Cardinal de Richelieu', for example, a Gallica, said to be the oldest of garden roses, and the opulent *R.* 'Charles de Mills', which fades to old purple. The fragrant Damask rose *R.* 'Ispahan' is a clear pink, and then there is the boldly striped *Rosa Gallica* (Rosa Mundi) and the Bourbon *R.* 'Ferdinand Pritchard', whose colour looks like cream over summer pudding. These grand names are but a few in an admirable collection. They grow among tangled geraniums, tall iris swords and banked perennials, creating a timeless border.

Above the crossing paths, a trellis painted blue-grey is draped with the miniature pink climber *R.* 'Cécile Brünner', ivory *R.* 'Prosperity', a Hybrid Musk rose and, needless to say, *R.* 'Félicité et Perpétue'! The Confederate-blue-grey paint was introduced into the garden by its creator, a lady from the southern United States. It is used on all of the garden furniture and trims, a personal expression of patriotism and roots.

Each quarter of this enclosed garden has a distinct personality. One is dominated by goblet-shaped apple trees, another by a cartwheel made from a collection of tightly clipped yellow and green box, its curves enclosing weeping mulberries. A third is spiked with the corkscrew shapes of clipped box and the fourth is the true potager. It is filled with vegetables, herbs and flowers which radiate like the spokes of a bicycle wheel from an aged quince tree.

These gardens were designed by the late Nancy Lancaster, an influential interior designer of the twentieth century. A scion of the formidable American Langhorne sisters, she was inspired to come to England by her aunt, Nancy Astor, England's first female Member of Parliament to take her seat.

At the end of her long life, Nancy Lancaster moved into the coach house at Haseley Court, directing the garden from here and guiding the new chatelaine, Fiona Haywood, passing on her inspiration to another receptive gardener. When you walk into the garden today, you will not notice any radical changes, and yet the garden has not been frozen in time. The ethos is there, but new plants and new plant combinations have been woven into the existing design, giving new life to a brilliant creation.

Nancy Lancaster planted the quince tree over fifty years ago. It stands in the thick elephant ears of bergenia that

Opposite: The spreading arms of the quince tree embrace the circular potager.

Below: Woven cloches form an unusual framework for beans to trail over.

has clusters of waxy bells on stiff tall stems in spring. The wide branches then shade a round grass path, which is in turn encircled by a large round bed divided by four paths, their edges abandoned to soft clouds of feverfew, wild chamomile and *Tanacetum parthenium*, with its masses of tiny, white, golden eyed, daisy-like flowers.

Chives, *Allium schoenoprasum*, are used as a permanent planting, their solid lines and clover-like flowers absolutely defining the spokes of the wheel. The precise lines of chives radiate from wavy sea kale, tiny wild strawberries and the glowing stems of ruby chard. More rigid spokes of green and yellow ginger mint and the deep golden marjoram, *Origanum vulgare* 'Aureum', capture the sunshine of summer. White horehound, *Marrubium vulgare*, a tough plant said to be one of the bitter herbs of the Feast of the Passover, completes the wheel.

Tall stands of grey cardoons rising out of soft *Salvia sclarea* break up the precision of the radiating spokes, which are finally captured in a soft tyre of mown grass, a restful circle of green providing access to the beds.

New beds strike out, breaking the horizontal rhythm with vertical tripod towers of sweet peas, that can be almond pink 'Kiri te Kanawa', carmine 'Nanette Newman', deep maroon 'Balmoral' and shaded lavender 'Titan' with rich purple 'Sue Pollard'. Each tower, clothed in flowers of a single colour, stands between poles of runner beans: 'Painted Lady' with bi-colour flowers, stringless 'Red Knight' which guarantees an abundant crop and the soft yellow 'Corona D'Ora', a pencil thin, climbing French bean. Each season the original design alters slightly to allow for crop rotation.

Line upon line of vegetables fill the large, outer beds. Often, two or three varieties of each vegetable are planted. 'Sugar Snap' and early cropping 'Green Shaft' peas grow close to 'Snow White' celeriac, grown for winter comfort, and purple sprouting broccoli, for a March harvest. Flowers such as *Limnanthes douglasii*, a sprawling, light green, ferny plant smothered with tiny yellow and white shiny flowers,

Below: The tall arms of the architectural cardoons reflect the confederate grey of the garden's buildings.

Left: Seedheads of garlic awaiting harvest.

break up the rows of productive plants. Unfortunately, it becomes a disgusting mess in late spring, but by mid summer its territory is commandeered by nasturtiums and the self-seeding *Nigella* 'Persian Night'.

This is not just another fantasy potager. Essential vegetables, such as the potatoes 'Red Duke', 'Charlotte', 'Nicola' and 'Desirée', are grown, along with the magenta-red onion 'Red Baron' and homely parsnips.

To the despair of the family rabbit, the leaf vegetables are enclosed by two smart pavilions. The sides of these structures are made of black mesh, stretched from a central pole and buried for 60cm (2ft). A curved pineapple, the symbol of hospitality, tops the structure, but its message is not directed at the rabbits. Inside the pavilion winter purslane grows, along with the bitter endive, chicory 'Bianca di Milano', pak choi, the butter-head lettuce 'Continuity' and 'Palla rossa'. Lines of spring onions

and rosy radishes give a red highlight to the beds, along with leaves of wild spinach.

The old walls of the garden hold and capture summer heat, and the gravely soil is suited to sun-loving plants. However, the long periods of English rain have been too much for the lavenders, and they have been replaced by teucrium, with soft, grey leaves clipped to create perfect hedges. Fiona has chosen *Teucrium chamaedrys*, a lovely, aromatic variety with rose-pink flowers, over the more usual *Teucrium fruticans*, which has stiff, silver foliage studded with French-blue flowers. More pinky-mauve has been added to the garden by stands of *Perovskia atriplicifolia* 'Blue Spire'.

Rarely do great gardens have the good fortune to slip into understanding hands, but as I leave Haseley Court, I know the best minds will always be focused on its care and it will remain one of England's most inspirational gardens.

Above: *Lavandula* 'Munstead' lettuce and onions
in perfect formation.

Beside Bloomingdale's escalators in New York, silver letters, spelling out the name of a trend-setting New York designer, glitter along the walls. Working in a sharp, 'tomorrow' style with a savvy that's particularly New York, this designer, I was told, was also passionate about gardening. She was mentioned as the creator of a potager in the French style – an idealised interpretation of a style that is already highly romantic. The following day, passing along the winding roads and picture-book towns and villages of New England, I was eager to see how this high priestess of New York fashion would interpret the European tradition of the *jardin potager*, high in the Connecticut hills.

An oblong, walled garden nestles into the protective curve of the hill, trusting in the land's protection from the severity of North American winters. On the crest of the hill, a rolling park occupies front row seats for a view across miles of undulating mountain tops. On the leeward side of the hill, the potager is a separate creation, totally divorced from the rest of the garden in both thought and design.

This garden is lavished with attention, taste, money and continuous love. It has the cosseted, privileged style of an exquisite beauty, pampered, constantly tended and its every need anticipated. Some people might describe it as 'a gem', but gems are hard and shiny and this garden is clothed in luminous, soft colours and rounded shapes, like minute pearls, with contented plants carefully screened from predators.

# A PRIVATE GARDEN
# UNITED STATES

Heavy, timber gates open on to the central, grassy allée of the quadrant garden, with its cruciform paths. The hinges of the gates were crafted locally by monks, made to resemble the gnarled branches of an ancient tree. The central axis is lined with tall, silver pear trees, pruned in the image of the poplars along French country roads and growing from an abundant sea of *Nepeta* 'Six Hills Giant' and *Iris germanica*. The cross axis of the garden is a tunnel slowly being engulfed by clematis, the pale pink 'Comtesse de Bouchaud' and French-blue 'Pearl d'Azur'. The clematis trail through *R.* 'New Dawn', a modern Climber whose blush-pink flowers deepen on vigorous and healthy branches, and *R.* 'White Dawn,' its close relation. The white clematis 'Marie Boisselot' thrives among the small white flowers of the rambling *R.* 'Sea Gull' and *R.* 'Félicité et Perpétue,' with its pompoms of creamy-white flowers born in large, fragrant clusters just touching the blue and white lavenders that billow at their feet. A stray 'Cupani' sweet pea grows above clumps of *Salvia farinacea*. The flowers of 'Cupani', first found growing wild in 1699, are deep magenta and violet blue, with a haunting fragrance. The salvias are the deep blue 'Victoria' and the silver-white 'Silver' – velvety plants that will tolerate heat, humidity and dryness. The depth of colour provided by the salvias and sweet peas saves the pastel confection from being too sugary sweet.

Below: free-form onion sculpture conquers the vegetable patch

Following page: parsley edges hold back a dozen verities of lettuce now at perfection, with the standard *Rosa* 'The Fairy'

Above: Apples espaliered as diamond trellis cover the substantial walls.

To one side of the flourishing arch are small beds arranged in groups of four. They are rimmed by broad hedges of trimmed box and packed with small mounds of the densely-petalled blooms of R. 'Little White Pet', the tiny modern shrub rose that is a sport of R. 'Félicité et Perpétue'. They grow around antique, iron parasols, the most delicate of garden ornaments. At one end a wisteria swathes a lion fountain, while stone balls make finials above the box shapes.

The garden's grid subdivides again, this time into wedges, around a group of four of the soft pink standard rose 'The Fairy', echoing the petite forms of the garden.

Eleven varieties of lettuce grow in the potager, including 'Cocade', a bronze-red heritage variety, 'Lolla Rossa', with its crimson, frilled mounds, and the green romaine lettuce 'Romulus'. Then there is the bitter, crunchy radicchio 'Rossan', tolerant of heat and very fast growing, and the endive 'Frisée', the most lacy of garden greens. This grows beside my favourite lettuce – a cos called 'Freckles' which has splashes of red frost on its green leaves.

There is a herb tapestry encircled by the broad leaves of 'Catalogno', the true Italian parsley. French tarragon, large-leaf marjoram and summer savory fill this garden with potential for the exacting cook who demands a wide variety of flavours and textures.

Bent hoops of iron and lines of fine wire capture the feathery fronds of asparagus that grow in their own, long patch. Tall, bronze fennel rises out of mid-summer's golden coreopsis. Nearby, tall, rusty tripods are being claimed by the candy-pink and white sweet pea 'Painted Lady', another heritage variety which dominates square beds fringed in shiny 'Purple Ruffles' basil and fine-foliaged, matching cosmos. Tall, fine cosmos makes sheer green films of single daisies throughout the garden. There is the deep magenta 'Carmine', the fairy-pink and white 'Pink Eye' and 'Radiance', a deep purple-red with a yellow eye. They flower above the 'Munstead' lavender, claiming the precisely paved paths.

Long lines of timber and string supports capture literally yards of climbing plants, including peas and a most esoteric collection of beans. 'Andrew Kent', the big red and brown blotched kidney bean, is there, along with the ivory and red pods of 'Tongue of Fire', 'Cannellini' a white kidney bean for minestrone soup, and the French flageolet 'Flambeau', to be found in classic cassoulet. Bumper crops are promised by the light green runner 'Meralda', growing beside 'Red Knight', which attracts humming birds to its red pea flowers.

Forty different types of new tomato plants are carefully tied to identical poles. 'Black from Tula', actually a purple-brown Russian heirloom, looks very similar to 'Russian Black', which is available in other countries. A new variety with the fetching name of 'Orange Strawberry' bears a brilliant, orange, heart-shaped fruit which the grower says is superb with basil and mozzarella. A thumbnail tomato called 'Ruby Pearl' bears tiny fruits in clusters of around fifteen. It is used as a garnish.

At the feet of the tomatoes grow a changing selection of vegetables. Sometimes there are the handsome French leeks 'St Victor' or the baby 'Albinstar' leeks. Aubergines came in the puce and white 'Rosa bianca' or the classic, bulbous, black 'Diva'. Permed heads of broccoli, ferny 'Bolero' carrots, or the crunchy fennel bulbs 'Romy' are all there, for this is a serious collection of vegetables.

For oriental cuisine, lines of Asian leaf plants are grown. There is the Japanese mustard mizuma, a flowering pak choi called 'Autumn Poem', and the black-green leaves of tatsoi. For flamboyant garnishes there are two kales: 'Red

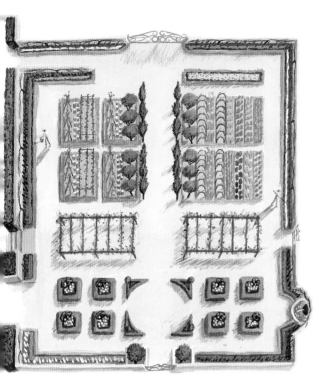

and yet in style, intention and result it is a *jardin potager*. It is an immaculate interpretation belonging to the glossiest magazines, but it is also a thoughtful selection of beautifully grown produce, which I am sure would command admiration and respect from one of Villandry's creators, herself an American heiress.

Auction houses on both sides of the Atlantic supplied a most romantic collection of objets d'art to furnish this potager garden. A line of venerable putti, whose beauty should assure them a place of honour, guard huge, open bins of compost, soil and manure. It is a strange combination, hinting of wild extravagance, but why not add a dash of decadence to this very functional part of the garden?

I was most intrigued by the unrecognisable, swathed shapes packed into a garden shed. I looked at them blankly until I was gently told that every tree, statue and garden feature is carefully covered in thick coats of frost proof material in late autumn. The entire garden is packed away for four months each year, and this precaution ensures its survival each winter.

Below: Old roses and clematis are beginning to soften the fine iron arches in this Connecticut garden.

Below: Immaculate walls of stakes and string awaiting the tentacles of beans and tomatoes.

Peacock', with bouquets of deep burgundy feathers, and 'White Peacock', iced white over an iced green band in early spring.

Each season the latest and best seed catalogues are digested. A mixture of heritage and new varieties, selected for trial and consumption, are planted with companion lines of the marigolds 'Lemon Gem' and 'Tangerine Gem', golden spotlights under the heavy green vegetables. The faded blue of Larkspur 'Blue Cloud' creates a touch of the old-fashioned garden in this New-World garden perfection.

Five different varieties of pears and forty-five of apples are espaliered within the walls. Above wide beds of shrubs, perennials and annuals, many now in tones of rich mauve and burgundy, make a more sophisticated impression than the original pastel shades.

Native American field flowers, such as the paper thin Californian poppy 'Ivory Castle', and brown eyed rudbeckia anchor this designer's garden firmly in its American soil,

Below: Miniature water lilies cover the small pond now the golden sacred koi have been banished.

Opposite: Artichokes awaiting harvest in late October.

If a small part of Australia could be called 'a green and pleasant land' it would be the rounded hills and valleys that lie about two hours to the south-west of Sydney. Tall stands of eucalyptus, reminiscent of bronze-grey clouds in the morning light, still clothe the hill tops. Beside the roads there are manicured paddocks where herds of dairy cattle graze, unaware that they are a threatened species. The threat to their existence comes from a sea of green grapes that is engulfing the countryside. Everywhere, tight, silver wires are erected to support more and more vines, planted to swell the ocean of Australian wine.

In the nineteenth century, colonial governors and industrialists rejoiced in the cool beauty of this area. They left a legacy of established trees and gardens in the English style. Kennerton Green, near Mittagong, lies on a country road in the heart of the area. Its history, typical of older Australian gardens, dates back to colonial days. With its wide lawns and exotic trees, vegetable plots and brick-edged beds, it was a transplanted, traditional English garden.

The original Kennerton Green's practical vegetable plot was enclosed by chicken wire stretched across metal pipes. This structure was erected by a previous owner after flocks of beautiful but devastating native birds had systematically devoured complete crops of strawberries and raspberries.

When I planned my potager at Kennerton Green, over eight years ago, I was still under the spell of Villandry, enthralled by the romance of medieval symbolism. Well

# KENNERTON GREEN

## AUSTRALIA

Clockwise from left: The leaves of Red Drumhead cabbages echo the colours of chives; grapes and passion fruit arches frame the small, central fountain; rainbow chard.

read in the potager tradition, I chose a cruciform layout, crossed again by the cross of Saint Andrew, with sensible flat paths of white gravel bordered with small box hedges. The paths all radiated from a decorative pond where a small metal putto plays beneath a fountain. The water rains on to miniature, pink water lilies. For a time, golden fish darted beneath the smooth, flat waterlily leaves, but their tendency to burrow down among the plant roots made the pond cloudy and they were sent to join the sacred Koi in the Rose Garden pool.

Eight standard roses form a circle around the central pond. 1.5–1.8m (5–6ft) in height, they are all small-flower varieties in whites and pinks, a selection that pays homage to the medieval cult of the Virgin Mary. The roses flower until early November each year, although the modern *Rosa* 'Bonica', a small, pink flower, is still in bloom on Christmas Day.

Two weeping, standard roses of the grafted rambler *R.* 'Francis E. Lister' guard the main entrance. Their small, single flowers are rimmed with pink, a style of rose that I am comfortable with here.

Kept firmly clipped into balls, the tall, dramatic shapes of the roses are echoed by the clipped lavenders. Most lavenders enjoy this climate, but *Lavandula* x *allardii* really thrives. Clipped as standard pompoms, it becomes the most spectacular plant, with 5cm (2in) spikes of stiff, violet-blue stems. However, the heads become so large and burdened by flowers that, unless they are well staked, they will snap in the wind. A firm prune after their flowering in summer minimises this problem. Lavenders were always included in the monastic garden, for their flavour and strong perfume. Along with roses, they have become essential elements in this garden. It is not just their medieval connotations that recommend

them, or their perfume which attracts pollinating bees. Their value also lies in the height they bring to this essentially flat garden design. They provide a second story of interest without creating great blocks of shade.

The brightly painted, wooden tripods for the beans and sweet peas also add height to the garden. Sweet peas hate wet years. When rainfall is high, their seeds will often refuse to germinate, or the young plants will sit there, sulking. Fear not, for as soon as the clouds part they will romp away, fighting the beans for dominance on the tripods.

The dark purple bean 'Purple King' has a long history in Australia. Its colour makes it highly desirable, and it is easy to grow. Seed catalogues refer to its insect repellent powers, but it nurtures snails like every bean I've ever planted.

Smaller tripods support peas. I am especially fond of the purple-podded Dutch peas ('*Capucyna*') grown not only for their excellent, shelled peas, but also for the two shades of blue flower that they produce.

Each year I say that I will not to grow cucumbers as they suffer so appallingly from mildew. Planting the mildew-tolerant varieties, however, offers some hope of success in our climate. The green 'Burpless' is a good variety. Tying it to a tripod or trellis allows the air to circulate and gives space for the fruit to form freely. This treatment gives the plants a sporting chance against mildew.

I also use architectural plants to give height to the garden. The high, thistle-like arms of the artichoke are vital, and their tall, globe-shaped buds tipped in purple burst into lavender thistles if not cut back. *Helianthus annus*, the simple sunflower, grows from 2.5–3.5m (7–11ft) in every shade from lemony-white to bronzy-brown, their seeds are beloved by wild birds and chickens alike. I also plant hollyhocks, *Alcea rosea*. When it is grown tightly along a border the hollyhock is prone to rust, but, in the open space of a potager, sun and wind dispel moisture and the flowers are especially beautiful. I am particularly fond of the chocolatey-purple ones, with petals like satin sheets.

I remember towering plants covered with maroon, plush bell pulls from my childhood. They were *Amaranthus caudatus*, the tassel flower, which self-seeded in the paths and beds of Australian country gardens. They provide splashes of hot colour and height to soften the grid design and a late summer giant to follow the tall, oriental poppies.

As I became ever more obsessed by the potential of the potager style, I played with mixing the colours of vegetables, herbs and flowers to create swathes of saturated colour from late winter to autumn, using successive planting in one dominant colour tone. I love the Brussels sprout 'Ruby', a winter remnant, with its purple-blue leaves and maroon, button sprouts, planted beside the purple-black 'Black Parrot' tulip. Tulips carry the height among new sets of red onions, creating a succession of vertical leaf shapes. Soon lines of 'Dragon Tongue' beans, long snakes of cream

Below: Peacocks, doves, pigeons and chickens patrol the gardens set among the eucalyptus clad hills of the southern highlands of New South Wales.

splashed with purple, have their toes tickled by *Viola tricolor* or heartsease, with its tiny, pansy faces of purple and gold. This is the flower that put Titania to the sleep and caused all the confusion:

> *And maidens call it, Love-in-idleness.*
> *Fetch me that flower; the herb I show'd thee once:*
> *The juice of it on sleeping eyelids laid*
> *Will make or man or woman madly dote*
> *Upon the next live creature that it sees.*
> A MIDSUMMER-NIGHT'S DREAM

A spring self-seeder, heartsease can be cleared away for aubergines, the purple speckled 'Lustadia di guardia' or the polished 'Long Purple', that can grow above ruffled purple basil. A mixture of burgundy leaves includes the Italian 'Lollo Rosso', a tutu of red bronze on a green skirt, and the totally red 'Red Velvet'.

I try to plant recipe ingredients together. Last summer ratatouille was on the menu. 'Black Krims' grew near the charcoal coloured 'Black Russian', 'Grosse Lisse', large, red and luscious, and 'Yellow Delicious', all varieties of tomato. Aubergines, onions and peppers and fifteen different varieties of basil made Sunday lunch easy.

All my plants are corralled within small walls of herbs. Rosemary, with fine needles of grey, aromatic leaves, will clip well into miniature hedges, with the bonus of clear blue flowers in spring. Santolina's ferny leaves prefer to be cut as a ball, but will produce a hedge if cut regularly, although it hates competition from neighbouring plants. Chives, form small, vertical palisades of regularly cut, fine, green-grey leaves that sport masses of round, mauve flowers.

Against a low wooden fence enclosing tiny hedges. summer fruits, peaches, nectarines, plums and apricots are neatly espaliered. The glory of the garden are 1.8m (6ft) high walls of apples, espaliered to form horizontal line upon line of picture-book apples in February. Luther said 'Even if I knew certainly that the world would end tomorrow, I would plant an apple tree today'. I agree with him.

I have planted two varieties of red apples, 'Red Delicious', an excellent eating apple and 'Jonathan', which cooks well too. This culinary balance has proved irrelevant, as the true joy of the trees comes from the near solid line of colour created by the apples, where the Mountain Lowry, a deep blue and scarlet parrot, becomes drunk on the fruit. He and hundreds of his friends, especially the brilliant red and green King Parrots, behave as though they have signed contracts to eat all of the fruit by mid-March.

A potager attracts birds with its flowers, seed heads and fruit. For me this is a bonus, especially when I turned to my spade one day to find a Kookaburra in charge of the handle and eyeing a worm at my feet.

Below: A sailor duck guards the barn entrance.

Opposite right: A grey wooden owl observes the Sluder potager in New York state.

Opposite below: *Achillea* 'Parkers Verity', *Phlox drummondii* in Mrs Sluder's flowering potager.

For days we had zigzagged along the east coast of America, a copy of *The Garden Conservancy Guide* to hand, along with notes from helpful friends. Our goal was to find the American interpretation of the *jardin potager*.

On balmy July evenings, after a generous American supper, we would take a walk through the streets of the nearest small town. Here fireflies often danced beyond the freshly painted white picket fences of small family gardens. These were planted with simple rows of seasonal vegetables, an apple tree, perhaps, with a forgotten tool or discarded pots and punnets lying beside the latched gate. These gardens represented an unconscious enjoyment of the *jardin potager* style. The simple rows of plants were designed to fill a family's requirements and tended at leisure. Many had not yet been planted for the summer season, but an occasional cabbage lingered on, often strangled by the morning glory vine, *Ipomoea versicolor*, with its trumpets of lavender, white and blue, or a blanket of sunshine-coloured *Nasturtium tropaeolum*.

Late one afternoon we drove down a country road through wooded hills. Under dense, spreading, deciduous trees we found a petite, French style manor house, with outbuildings, courtyards and gardens joined by walls with decorative finials and dovecotes. In geometric gardens of monochromatic green, shade-loving plants, Mr and Mrs McCausland told the story of their potager, which only fifteen years before had been a tomato field. The McCauslands are self-confessed francophiles, with a house

brimming with souvenirs of many trips to France and a fine library of garden books. It was from these two sources that the design for the garden developed. The remaining inspiration came from Russell Page's *Education of a Gardener*. His influence is expressed in the composition, where precise design falls away to fields and stands of timber, but the vegetable garden is faithful to the French potager plan.

An informal, basketweave-patterned path linked the house to the potager garden, luring the visitor through a darkened tunnel of dense, crooked hazels to a rectangular field, now basking in the hot afternoon sunlight. Six oblong beds are cut sharply from the bright green lawn. They are fenced by four white corner posts supporting wires of espaliered 'Red Delicious' apples.

The beds are arranged in the traditional grid pattern, and the planting is in straight rows. The only exception to this military precision is the asparagus bed, filled with the tall, delicate, fern-like leaves of mature plants. (Mildew-resistant strains of asparagus are now widely available in nurseries, promising higher yields and long-lived crowns.) Burpee's deep purple asparagus spear 'Purple Passion' adds a colour bonus to the popular, greenish 'Jersey Knight'.

Another plot contains herbs and cutting flowers. Everyday choices for the house, these include the indispensable basil, flat-leaf and curly parsley, then stands of grey-green chives with cottage perennials and annuals. A deep purple-blue salvia and orange zinnias formed cheerful groups of simple colour. A line of lavender holds

# SMALL GARDENS OF THE UNITED STATES

back bushes of thin, light green lemon balm (*Melissa officinalis*) which gives off a lemon fragrance. Mounds of silver-grey sage, an essential herb for traditional stuffings, and lines of mid-summer lettuces were crowded by weather-tolerant marigolds. American turnip, smooth and white below the soil and with a purple line around its emerging leaves, and a Siberian or winter kale beside the blue-green leaves and hot pink veins of the 'Red Drumhead' cabbage have all found homes in this productive garden.

As it was 'bean time', climbing beans like 'Kentucky Wonder' were supported by stakes, and rows of small, bush beans were already producing. American seed catalogues offer a three-colour mix of bush beans, made up of green 'Slankette', creamy-yellow 'Roc d'Or' and burnished purple 'Royal Burgundy'. I plan to plant them next summer, combining them with the ultra-moody, purple leaves of the hot pepper 'Pretty in Purple' to create a witch's cauldron of purple, yellow, orange and scarlet.

Another plant rejoicing in deep, moody colours was the hyacinth bean 'Ruby Moon', with purple pods, shiny leaves and lavender and deep pink flowers, climbing vigorously over hooped arches in the McCauslands' garden. A visual knockout, with flowers, new leaves and pods, all completely edible, that would surely add unexpected variety to a summer's evening meal.

For overseas visitors, lost in admiration as they drive through the wooded hills of the eastern USA, the landscape evokes a strong sense of America's colonial past. The

neatly painted clapboard houses and the cheerful, fenced gardens conjure up tales of intrepid settlers. Settlers who must have cast anxious glances at the encircling woods, wary of their reception by the Native Americans and of the large, inquisitive, brown bears. Talking to many a devoted gardener, I realised that wary looks are still cast towards the woods. Hidden in dappled shade there are deer, squirrels, chipmunks and other wild creatures which make country gardening a hazardous adventure.

As I sat on a patch of shaded grass one summer's afternoon in upper New York State, I saw a deer quietly wander towards Mrs Sluder's flowering vegetable garden, a small rose parterre directly in its path. A grey squirrel hopped on to a post and chain fence, oblivious to our presence. An electric wire, safely hidden below long trails of rose and clematis, added a deterring punch to the fence. A patch of ripening sweetcorn was also well fenced to deter racoons. The first rows of corn were planted after the late frosts, and followed by five different varieties planted twenty-four days apart, with the late season, pearly white 'Silver Queen' well worth the ninety-two days it took to mature.

Oblong in shape and divided by a wide, grassed path, the potager is cut by long, rectangular beds into two mirror reflections. Half-moon parterre beds, separated like pieces of pie, lie at either end. One parterre holds a random selection of modern roses: firm favourites like *Rosa* 'Apricot Nectar', a fully fragrant Floribunda in tones of apricot yellow, and Meilland's most famous rose, the creamy-yellow Hybrid tea rose *Rosa* 'Peace', with *R.* 'Mister Lincoln', another Hybrid tea rose in crimson velvet. At the parterre's other end is a summer collection of perennials. There are the turned back, daisy petals of *Echinacea purpurea*, the puce cone flower and the stiff plates of brilliant yellow *Achillea* 'Parkers Verity' with ferny, silvergreen

foliage, a warm climate favourite for well-drained soils. Bold oriental lilies, with the coloured turbans of tiger lilies in yellows and oranges, add drama to the garden's careful formality. Other beds hold herbs at summer's end, rows of mop-head chives, grey and purple sage, rosemary and old lavender make a mockery of these defined spaces, but the most precise formation of canes holds row upon row of splendid tomatoes. This is not an esoteric collection of fashionable varieties, but an ensemble of all-American favourites. 'Fourth of July' promised 110g (4oz) of tomato by Independence Day. The main crop was the ever dependable 'Big Beef', supplemented by the large, pink heirloom 'Brandy Wine', another American staple. The 'Viva Italia' hybrid is a sauce and bottling choice, and the vigorous, climbing, 'Sweet 100 Plus' offers a cascade of bite-size fruit.

As in any good country garden, vegetables are planted in a no-nonsense rotation. Snap peas go in by March and are cropped and removed by 4 July. A succession of lettuces and beans are planted with peppers of all shapes and sizes. There are the long, crinkled, cayenne chillies 'Turkish Sweet', that have been likened to Aladdin's slippers. The elongated chartreuse-coloured 'Bananaroma' is also there. It often reaches 20cm (8in) and is ideal for pickling. The dark red-green hot chilli 'Poblano' is planted in place of the volcanic 'Biker Billy', said to be the fiercest of all.

*Helianthus debilis*, the white Italian sunflower, is a multi-stemmed old variety of custard-lemon petals around coffee-brown centres. A 2m (6ft) mainstay of flowering kitchen gardens, it is soaking up the summer sun.

Surrounded by native woods, the potager stands in a grass clearing and is overlooked by comfortable tables and chairs on a paved patio. It is a delightful example of how an old European tradition can, as if by stealth, take over the American garden patch.

The paintings of Norman Rockwell gave the world a view of American life that was as folksy as an old sampler. It left us with a longing to see old rocking chairs standing on wooden verandas and tall, wooden, frame houses with fine old barns behind. As a result, the sight of a perfect, red-ochre barn with its windows painted snow white sent us into total ecstasy. Then we saw the garden and we screeched to a halt. The entire roadside and the perimeter of the vegetables patch was engulfed by an enormous band of Asiatic lilies in orange, gold and pink – a virtuoso display by the best lilies of the season.

We were not the first awed strangers to stop and ask to photograph the garden, and we were made very welcome. Honoured with the Lady Bird Johnson award for her contribution to beautifying America, the owner tends this paint-box garden alone, her flowers and vegetables, berries and vines forming an important part of her long life.

As the Asiatic lilies fade, ample clumps of day-lilies take over, creating an echo of the marmalade colours. This is a plant that seems to be totally in love with the variations of America's climate. In a Maryland garden, I saw day-lilies used as architectural swatches of flowers in huge blocks of colour designed by James van Sweden, and in mixed borders flowering profusely, but I have never seen them used more imaginatively than in the edging of this vegetable garden.

Tall plumes of pink and white astilbe will soon add height to the border and the white collars of Shasta daisy will create clear highlights with its snowy petals. As the season progresses, wandering pumpkins will climb the fence, their tendrils engulfing berries, fruits and flowers, and the small white and yellow buttons of feverfew will self-seed into the vegetable patch.

Sturdy tomato plants were heavily mulched with straw and lines of summer herbs and vegetables were late starters in this cool valley in the Connecticut hills. Truthfully this garden was not a true potager, but its imaginative use of colour and plant material could inspire another *jardin potager* maker to abandon tried and true edging favourites and experiment with the vertical shapes of a rainbow such as this.

Previous page: A decorative fence pannel overlooks the potager Stonecrop, New York state.

Above and right: A virtuoso display of colour, as tall Asiatic lilies edge this roadside vegetable garden.

Opposite: The verdant potager at Stonecrop.

# CHAPTER 5
## A PERSONAL
## APPROACH

In every walk of life there are those with the style to walk to 'the beat of a different drum', who see further, defend their own convictions or simply dare to try another approach. This is a good description of the gardeners in this section. Each of them has created a garden that is a very personal interpretation of the traditional potager style. The gardens express a personal philosophy or an individual style, some discarding many of the accepted norms. The psychology of the gardener is more important here than the plants themselves.

There are some gardens that overpower with their grandeur, and others do it through sublime beauty. When you meet Bob Ray you forget all that. His garden simply brings a great big smile of happiness to your face. Not far from Annalopolis, near Chesapeake Bay in Maryland, USA, it is an unselfconscious expression of personal passion.

It was not so long ago that Bob decided to build a garden on a patch of abandoned land beside a car park, simply because he felt he needed to. Part American Indian, Bob wanted to go back to his roots. He felt that he could heal the scars of a chequered career through the rhythm of the seasons, and he knew that the methodical routine of garden chores can restore an inner peace.

A man of the land, Bob knew intuitively that his plot of earth was dead and spent. That is why he moved in 380 truck-loads of soil and manure to nourish his new plants. Then he planted a collection of fruit trees to protect the fledgling garden from adventuresome hot rodders experimenting with their wheels in the gritty car park next door. To form a barricade against the encroaching woods, Bob also planted a thick belt of cannas. Their deep bronze, paddle leaves now grow like an impenetrable tropical hedge, behind self-seeded bronze fennel, drifting like an open curtain, a skeleton silhouette of burnished tone catching any movement in the sticky air.

'Critters', great and small, are Bob's preoccupation. Loved and despaired of, they must be accommodated in the garden's cycle. Bob reasons that by spraying the very tall cannas with a systemic pesticide he catches 'them' before they come down into his tiny seedlings and create havoc each spring.

Bean beetles and tomato worms are given a bed to themselves, for Bob figures they will not move into uninfected garden beds if they are adequately provided for. Similarly

Below: Green peppers grow abundantly in the steamy warmth of mid summer Maryland.

Opposite: Dark leafed cannas attempt to hold back the approaching forest.

rabbits, the curse of many a garden, if provided with the clover and sky blue chicory that they adore, will ignore other succulent leaves. All 'critters' can be organised, even the hovering hawk catches the tiny field mice now that the cat has decided to retire.

Like many a traditional *jardin potager*, all of the plants are crammed into a rectangular grid of beds. The central space is now a vine-covered lattice tunnel, where a garden seat is provided as a place to rest or soak up the energy given off by the thriving garden. For this garden bursts with vigour, and the plants grow enormously tall in the steamy summer sunshine.

The central tunnel is host to a great collection of plants. Climbing right to the top is the runner bean 'Kentucky Wonder' with its very long green pod. It is a well-loved variety, widely used in many American gardens. Further down the trellis the cherry tomato 'Sweet Million' likes to be espaliered. A heavy cropping variety, it is grateful to have support, and even in this humid atmosphere it is quite disease resistant.

Around the tiny tomatoes rise the glowing red stems of the Swiss chard 'Rhubarb', providing another tone of red with the strident orange-yellow tomato 'Golden Nugget' keeping it company. Ripening in mid-July, this is an extremely good mannered plant as it doesn't crack or drop off the bush.

Within nodding distance on the tunnel's other side, the mint-green 'Nevada' lettuce, densely interplanted with sweet basil, hugs the ground. Vigorous climbing gourds, soon to be covered with their hard-shell fruits, ripen into bulbous shapes. They were treasured by the American Indians who dried and split them, turning them into useful dippers.

Bob's strong, healthy plants seem to capture you with

# BOB RAY'S GARDEN
## UNITED STATES

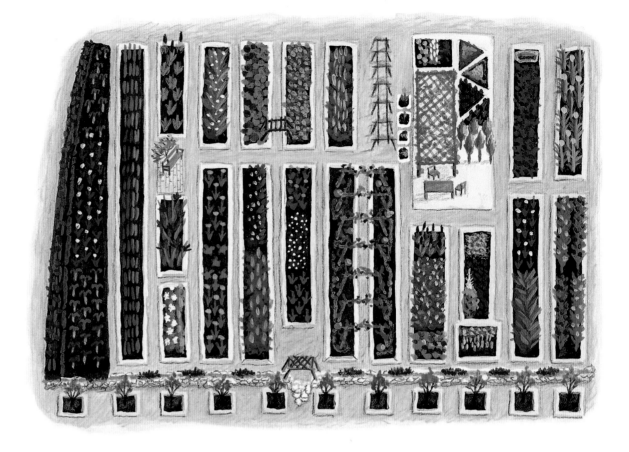

Opposite: Pink Asiatic *Liliums* and gladioli provide pools of summer colour in Bob Ray's gardens.

their rampant vitality, engulfing the senses with their imaginative bursts of colour. Deep purple aubergines, planted once the daytime temperature hits 27°C (80°F), look like polished American gridirons. A new variety, 'Black Bell', produces glossy black fruit, while baby 'Bambino' bears walnut size fruits from lavender-blue flowers. These rich, midnight colours were planted beside magenta echinacea (the cone flower) a tall, stiff, native of the American prairie. Drought resistant and cold hardy, echinacea is known for its herbal properties. Once established, it flowers from mid-summer. Daisy-petalled skirts surround an auburn head until autumn's end, if it is given full sun. Here, beside the regal toned aubergines, they create a royal mixture of colour and contrasting shapes.

That totally red bird, the native American cardinal darted from the sky to the golden petals of a giant sunflower. Already shooting skywards, Bob assured me that his sunflowers reach 4 m (14 ft) with blooms up to 75 cm (30 in) wide. His giant is called 'Gigantus', a true garden colossus which even outgrows the 'Russian Sunflower'. As we stood in this sunflower forest, a furry squirrel scampered up the sturdy stem. I could well believe Bob's account of cutting them down with his chainsaw at the end of the season.

Crammed tightly together, hundreds of spikes of knicker-pink and strident yellow Dame Edna-type gladioli were terminated by equally vigorous and brilliant Asiatic lilies. Calypso coloured, square petalled zinnias and feathery asparagus were grown in long blocks, as were the dinner-plate blooms of the perennial hibiscus, with

its silken faces of clotted cream, pink and burgundy. Like the trumpet lily of the hemerocallis, these flower just for the day. Nearby, white cosmos and lavender-blue larkspur move as mist in the breeze.

Strong orange and red trailing nasturtiums and old-gold coreopis, a wild flower of the American continent, had haphazardly self-seeded. This prompted Bob's best story: 'They are like gorillas, they sleep where they want to.' Definitely the best description I've ever heard of wilfully self-seeding plants!

Companion plantings were the garden's police force. Groupings of fine, tall dill waved above onions and strawberries, providing natural protection. Tall umbrellas of hogweed guarded the aubergines and the lavender. Other plants in Bob Ray's 'medicine' list were curly topped 'Forest' parsley and flat-leaf, sweet Italian parsley planted around the leaves of 'Red Drumhead' cabbage to fend off fluttering white moths. The remains of last season's onions and leeks had to be kept away from the new-season vegetables, as bugs had already affected them. Bob believes in putting plants that complement each other in the kitchen close together in the garden as well. Consequently basils, green and purple, were planted with sturdy capsicums and tomato plants, fine dill covered the cucumbers and coriander was planted alongside beans.

To one side of the plot, nearly concealed by lines of Indian corn, travelling pumpkins and honey yellow squash, a tall Indian tepee stood, looking out across its own garden. Built by Bob, it centres around a well-used fire pit. Here Bob, filled with the spirits of his Cherokee ancestors, expounded his ideals about the co-existence of man and nature.

There is a figure in Indian mythology who has special powers of fertility and germination. He is portrayed by many Indian tribes as a 'hunch backed flute player'. His hump contains the seeds that he scatters to the winds and the flute is the spirit of the seeds. As I sat listening to Bob I remembered this story. His garden, although organised, is a free spirit tended as time allows. It is extraordinarily verdant and productive, obviously well and truly in tune with ancient beliefs.

There is a theory that seeds collected in the wild, stored and dried by traditional methods in earthenware pots or in plain maize rugs, hold their fertility for decades longer than the supermarket's 'small packets of aluminium'. Although this garden is the product of the USA today, the growing songs of Bob's forefathers still resonate in the air.

Bob is not trying to play tricks, his garden could not be anywhere but America in the twenty-first century. As we talked, large delivery trucks rumbled over the pot-holed car park to the adjoining restaurant, and the noise of a six-lane highway, with its string of fast food outlets, petrol pumps and convenience shops could be heard in the distance. The garden was a green buffer zone between the old culture celebrated by the tepee and the fast track ugliness of roadside USA. Within its green walls it shut out all competing points of view and concentrated on producing an abundance of fruit, flowers, vegetables and herbs.

Above: Bob Ray's wigwam surrounded by plants native to the Americas.

Opposite: *Echinacea purpurea,* used by native Americans as a medicinal plant.

Below: The garden supplies produce to the restaurant behind.

# HERONSWOOD
# AUSTRALIA

Below: Giant cabbages, 'Tuscan Black' kale, artichokes and the tall, gray herb *Artemisia* among edible violas and pot marigolds makes a potager of a decorative border.

For many Australians, the name Dromana conjures up memories of seaside holidays, old wooden beach shacks, crayfish, coastal tea trees and the four-day Melbourne weather cycle of a day of rain, a fine day, a day of boiling hot sun and a day of furnace strength winds. We knew that every fourth day of the holidays would be spent indoors playing Monopoly. Then we would spend three days at the beach, before cooling our sunburn when it rained again.

Soft hills descend to the sea. Over the years holiday cottages were upgraded and gracious summer residences

now command the best views. Heronswood, an imposing stone house built in the Gothic style, is surrounded by a historic garden. It was here in the late 1970s that Clive and Penny Blazey began assembling the seeds of all but forgotten cottage plants and rare vegetables, establishing Diggers Garden Club.

I was among a new generation of aspiring gardeners at that time, brimming with ideas but frustrated by the limited seeds and plants available to us in Australia. The Blazey's arrival was a most stimulating event in the world of Australian gardening. Here, at long last, were the coloured silver beets with stems of red, orange, yellow and pink that we had seen in European gardens. They had five colours of peppers and multiple types of tomatoes, enabling us to create more fireworks in our own potagers. They concentrated on smaller-growing and more piquant plant varieties. Clive's message was that commercial vegetables were grown for longer shelf life, rather than flavour and texture. He started to criticise pesticides, weed killers and synthetic fertilisers long before it became fashionable to do so.

Until the 1950s, Australia was peopled principally by colonialists of British descent. We ate meat and three vegetables, and the meat was the most important ingredient of any meal. It was even written firmly in the union rules that sheep shearers were not to be fed salad! Vegetables were always boiled, unless it was Sunday, when they were roasted and timed to be ready as the family walked in from church.

The advent of air travel broke the tyranny of distance, and the influx of European migrants after the Second World War transformed Australia. Now we wanted salad bowls filled with leaves of different colours, textures and shapes. We also needed the ingredients to make the dishes described in the newly popular glossy magazines. Clive's magazine became the adventurous gardener's bible!

The Blazeys made one of Australia's first potagers in the lawn at Heronswood. It was designed to show off the plants in their catalogue. Circular in shape, it was surrounded by a large curve of wooden trellis that contained the rampant pumpkins, gourds, squash and courgettes. Digger's Seeds supply twelve different kinds of pumpkin and squash. The collection includes 'Ironbark', our national icon, with its armoured shell of gun-metal green that you have to take an axe to. It is worth every grunt and groan for its flavour and texture. At the other end of the scale is the small 'Red Kuri' and spaghetti squash that falls from its shell as long pasta-like strands.

No Australian summer is complete without half a cantaloupe filled with ice cream. This warm-season crop, along with watermelon, can engulf an entire garden. The Blazeys widened our appreciation of cantaloupes. They offer the crocodile skinned 'Hales Best', and ten varieties to the Turkish 'Leopard Melon', which are like small, flecked yellow and green ovals from a Turkish bazaar.

To make the Heronswood potager, six segments were cut from the turf. The round shape was dissected by three crossed turf paths and long curving beds were placed at the base of the trellis. The idea of edging the beds with box was discarded as being too time consuming. Seasonal edging is used instead. Sometimes it is verdant parsley in spring, massed geraniums or non-sprawling nasturtiums in summer. I have visited the potager many times and it is always entirely different in colour, planting and mood, even tilled and fallow in winter its geometric shape and tiny St Fiacre statue pleases.

In high summer the outer trellised rim can contain tall stands of corn. Full sun allows the plants to mature easily,

Above: A masterpiece of planting for colour and texture in nurseryman Clive Blazey's *jardin potager*.

Right: A giant savoy cabbage claims top billing.

and the trellis gives protection from the nearby sea's damaging wind. Corn needs warm summers to germinate. It is planted in cool, temperate Melbourne between November and December, but nearer to the tropics it can be planted year round. The Digger's catalogue offers 'Slate Blue Popping Corn' and the white and yellow kernels of 'Breakthrough Honey and Cream' as well as 'Golden Bantam' and ornamental red Indian corns.

Runner and climbing beans demand space on the trellis too, away from sea breezes, while dwarf bean varieties tangle with *Tagetes patula* 'Lemon Gem', a fine marigold with lemon scented foliage.

The summer before last, as I looked along one of the wedge-shaped beds, I found my eye being carefully drawn from a rust red group of small violas, to the bright rounded green leaves of the cos lettuce 'Kerdi'. Slightly taller were the long, cool, green, oak leaf fingers of the Heirloom lettuce 'Royal Oak Leaf'. Then the wide, purple-blue leaves of cabbage were backed by the even taller leaves of the red stemmed silver beet. Finally these coloured leaves were topped by 1.5m (5ft) of the narrow, curly, slate

black leaves of the kale 'Tuscan Black'. It was a painter's masterpiece, revealing an understanding of each plant's growth, colour and form. It was a cook's delight, too, as it was a feast of edible leaves.

Giant vegetables escape from the tilled and trimmed formal potager to add surprise to the garden beds. Spruce blue 'January King' cabbages, with white-veined leaves around a rose-pink heart, complement tall, blue-grey artichoke leaves and large mounds of *Artemisia* 'Absinthium', a silver-grey hedging that must be controlled or it becomes very rank and unruly.

A high spot on the autumn garden calendar in Melbourne is the tomato festival hosted by the Blazeys. Clive offers perhaps the largest commercial selection of styles and varieties in Australia, all the tried and true varieties plus exotics like 'Yellow Pear', truly golden and pear shaped, 'Russian mixed', the seeds rescued from Eastern Europe and 'Green Zebra', which adds melon-like splashes of yellow and green to a garden.

For many years old cottage flowers, that loosen the rigid design of the traditional potager grid, were only available if a good friend carefully saved seeds, but they are now widely available. I had not known the lemon cosmos or the Mexican crepe poppy 'Argemore', which gives good height to break the flat planes of the potager, until I spied them in the Digger's Catalogue

Clive's message to gardeners is not restricted to the heritage plants he encourages us to rediscover and enjoy. He also encourages gardeners to save the seeds of plants we have always known, so they are not lost through our own laziness in purchasing everything we eat and plant. He asks Australians to collect and then improve the seeds of native, edible plants that were ignored by the European colonials. Thankfully, these plants have survived in the wild, although they pass unrecognised by most of us. Perhaps it is the duty of home gardeners to introduce them to the table, so that they become accepted like lemon grass, pak choi, snake beans and curled mustards, that have crossed over from Oriental cuisines into our own kitchens in less than two decades.

Clive maintains that selective breeding over hundreds of years has made traditional vegetables more disease resistant, so that they need fewer chemicals than hybrid, commercial varieties. He believes that our heritage vegetables should be our future, not genetically modified crops bred with pesticides and weed killers. Clive is forcibly leading Australian gardeners to honour their horticultural heritage, which he illustrates so ably each season in his captivating potager beside the sea.

Above: Historic Heronswood in Dromana, Victoria.

The moody grey-green of the garreque, the native plants that cover the hills and encircle both the château and its vineyard, has a feeling reminiscent of a majolica bowl.

Grapes have been grown in the shelter of these hills since Roman times. The walls surrounding the potager could be made from salvaged Roman stone and the giant grid of their layout reflects the geometric street plan of a Roman city or the ordered gardens that would have surrounded the fine Roman villa that once stood nearby.

The planting takes its colours from the warm, sun-baked tones of the local Provençal pottery. Its three main terraces are linked by a long iron tunnel, originally built in the 1850s to house an exotic collection of long legged ostriches. Moved to a new position, it now blazes with climbing roses in every shade of hot pink and orange. First choices were the modern climber *Rosa* 'Phyllis Bide', with its sprays of small, salmon flowers flushed with yellow. The dark pink *R.* 'Mrs Solvay' is among 180 repeat-flowering climbers, underplanted with an experimental collection of grasses, ranging in colour from burnt sienna to purple.

I saw the heat of a hot summer's day captured by apricot, marmalade and tango-pink roses that were completely encased in high borders of kniphofia, the red hot poker which stored the noon day fire in orange points, its long, thin leaves making a grey-green, impenetrable stockade. This unexpected grouping of plants is typical of the elegant and individual French style epitomised by Madame Chancel. She is a person who stamps her

# CHÂTEAU
# JOANIS

Opposite page: The grey green natural vegetation of Provence encircles the garden behind the old gate.

Left: The garden specialises in heritage tomatoes of the Mediterranean region.

Below: Lines of clipped santolina outline the ancient stones.

unique signature on whatever she does. A knowledgeable plantswoman, she has a complete understanding of the extremes of the Mediterranean climate of her home near Aix-en-Provence. While winter temperatures can fall below freezing, plants must also face extreme summer heat and the season of the Mistral wind. The design of her *jardin potager* makes no concessions to accepted plant combinations. She revels in her position on the flip side of conventional wisdom, creating her own style, setting new trends.

Through high iron gates a purposeful, wide path of Roman stones merges with gravel from the River Durance. This forms the central axis of the garden, its sides seemingly riveted in place by pencil-thin Italian cypresses, looking like giant nails bolted to the earth by square washers. In reality, the washers are beds of clipped santolina, balls or spikes of *Lavandula* 'Grosso', a hardy and heat resistant variety, excellent for making lavender water, all squared up by low, clipped, box hedges.

The quadrant plan is bisected by narrow stone paths, often passing lines of apples and pears. These are French heritage varieties especially grafted on to rootstock suitable for cultivation in Provence. The red fruit creates a strong foil for the rows of scarlet chard planted directly beneath it, and for the tripods of twenty-five different types of tomatoes garnered from French and Italian catalogues. The collection includes curiosities from South America and Russian tomatoes from the Crimea that mature in thirty-five days.

A collection of twelve different cabbages and kales creates its own architecture in different tones of grey. The varieties include the 1m (3ft) high 'Black Hero', mixed with tall Swiss chard 'Giant of Nice'. Its curly,

bat-shaped leaves in the deepest green are fronted by lines of tightly clipped, pale grey santolina, which flourishes in the dry chalky soil. Behind is the bluest of grapes, *Vitis vinifera*. This is a triumph of colour, with leaves of vintage mulberry and claret shades which draw the whole colour composition together.

Elegant euphorbias grow all over the garden: the evergreen *Euphorbia characias wulfenii*, 1.2m (4ft) of soft grey leaves with flowers of a sharper green, and *Euphorbia* x *martinii*, which produces nearly red leaves, acid-green flowers and 1 m (3 ft) branches that give structure and drama to the garden, while tolerating its dry conditions.

There are monstrous walls of climbing beans, ready to be picked and tossed in the château's own olive oil. They are mulched with the black pips and grape waste discarded during wine making. When it is treated and mixed with

bark, it becomes the garden's caviar, a rich, black topping that gives the garden its lushness.

Seriously good horticulture sits happily beside the garden's *joie de vivre*. Early lettuces are protected by cloches that are replaced at the season's end by round, white stones, a joyous solution to bare space that causes amazement to garden visitors.

In solitary splendour, an oversized, antique, garden snail is a remnant of the garden kitsch of two centuries ago, another mischievous joke that is the product of a very original mind. The snail is enclosed by a circular wall of *Rosa* 'Zéphirine Drouhin', a fragrant Bourbon of a deep pink that appreciates the Mediterranean warmth and flowers continuously.

Other edges of the potagers are planted with lines of achillea, cut at least three times a year to create low walls of

Below: Clipped santolina balls resemble rounded nail heads, that seem to bolt the spikes of columnar cypresses to the earth.

fine, ferny leaves. Treated in this way, it flowers repeatedly, producing flat-headed flowers that seem designed to be seen from above. Against the translucent stems of rainbow chard, in scarlet, yellow, orange and pink, or perhaps the capsicum 'Sweet Chocolate', a vegetable of gloss purple-black grows behind hedges of perennial blue asters, again kept cut to around 75 cm (2 ft) creating walls of azure.

These detailed plantings lie on the potager terrace, beside the château. Roses and fruit trees are planted on the terrace above, and more fruit and ornamental trees on the one below. Although this is a modern garden, the château dates from the fourteenth century, appearing on the maps drawn by Catherine de Medici's cartographer, Cassini, and it has been continuously inhabited for generations.

The design of a new 'historic' potager opens up a host of possibilities. Here, however, they decided to create the garden of an eighteenth-century chatelaine, adopting a design that was still rooted in medieval thought. It was to be a garden that could supply the needs of a large household and a diverse community.

The writings of Pliny the Younger were consulted, as were Medieval herbals. A selection of medicinal and culinary herbs were drawn from these sources and are harvested to make a range of healing teas – fennel, chamomile, peppermint, lemon balm and coriander – to promote well-being. After a walk through this deeply satisfying garden, I felt them to be quite unnecessary.

The garden of Château Joanis could not have been created by anyone but Madame Chancel. In every respect this is a generous garden, for its size, architectural shapes and the abundance of its produce. It is sophisticated and chic, but much more, too, for it has the originality, warmth and sensual beauty of its maker. This beyond all others gardens I would take with me to my desert island!

Left: A nineteenth-century garden snail, a prize flea market find, provides pure fun in the potager.

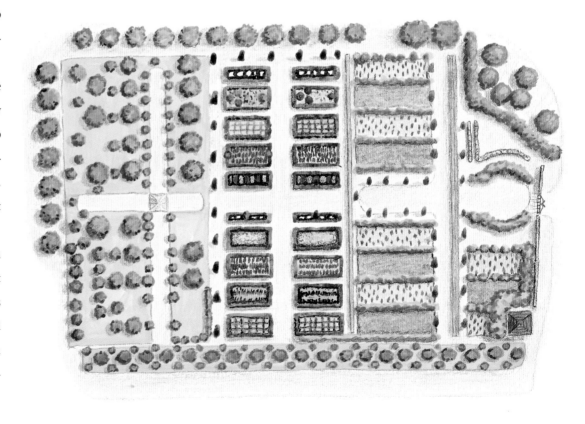

# CHAPTER 6
## FUTURE THOUGHTS

During the twentieth century, the grid garden of straight paths and square plots ceased to represent the pinnacle of fashion, and they beat a retreat to the utilitarian end of the garden. Many influenced the sweeping away of formality, including the Irish gardener and writer William Robinson, who promoted a naturalistic approach to design which ousted the formal garden at the end of the nineteenth century, and the American landscape architect Thomas Church, who created asymmetric designs all the rage in the 1940s. The potager has been the path to rediscovery for those uncomfortable with naturalism and asymmetry. It has allowed us to revive the basic, symmetric form, endowing it with a new bounty of curious and fascinating vegetables, herbs, fruits, strident flowers and even livestock.

Many new potager gardens hark back to the past. They are made by those fortunate enough to own land and can largely ignore innovation. However, the bitter truth is that the majority of people who would like to garden live in an urban world, where their only claim to space is a balcony, a rooftop, or a tiny patch of the inner-city soil.

In 1999, the organisers of the international garden festival at Chaumont-sur-Loire, near Blois in France, invited a selection of garden designers, architects, sculptors and painters to explore the concept of the potager in the twentieth century. The results were often bizarre, sometimes witty, but never predictable. Some participants took all elements of the potager, while others restricted themselves to a few features, choosing settings that ranged from urban environments to the plains of India.

The potager designed for an itinerant city dweller was planted in a collection of recycled oil drums. These were painted in reds, greens and blues, and clustered together on a graffiti-scrawled floor. These industrial containers were filled with the romantic components of the

Below: Mechanised nostalgia, as computerised watering cans provide a fun alternative to watering drudgery.

Right: Plant labels became colourful features in their own right.

Below: The aroma of mint in the noon day sun was captured by the dense hornbeam hedges in this potager inspired by a Persian poem at Chaumont-sur-Loire.

Top: An environmentally friendly garden shed.

Above: Broken pottery was a suggested option for adding colour and texture to a garden path.

traditional potager. One drum was filled with water and waterlilies to represent a pond. The purple basil 'Purple Opal', trailing beans 'Beurre Neckargold' and 'Coco Rouge de Prague', the artichoke 'Salanquet Violet', fennel, white nicotiana, the tomato 'Tumbler', spiky crocosmia, all the familiar potager staples, filled the other drums to create a luxurious garden from reprocessed materials.

Every conceivable vegetable and herb were contained in table-top gardens, along with brilliant, scattered flowers. These gardens were raised beds on legs. The plants were encouraged by adjustable greenhouse glass and shade screens, with built-in trellis to contain the climbing plants. An adaptation of the raised garden, they were waist high, square, regularly placed, a single unit easily moved from balcony to hospital or rooftop.

A romantic potager inspired by a Persian poem was built in a small courtyard. It was enclosed by dusty pink *Tamarix pentandra* 'Rubra' trees, plantings of the carmine coloured rose *R.* 'Chartreuse de Parme' and *R.* 'Jardin de Villandry', plain and variegated mint, pungent white-lace coriander, *Cleome* 'Violet Queen' – a matching carmine colour repeated yet again by *Mirabilis jalapa* 'Tea Time' and *Pelargonium* 'Attar of Roses'. A grid of shallow, pottery bowls of floating petals stood beside an Arabic pattern of moving water. The sharp, clean fragrance of mint predominated in the midday heat, but the perfume of the roses engulfed the senses when evening fell.

There was another potager of great panache. It was a cube that opened out as a cross to make four stilted sundecks. Some were sheltered by smart white canvas, and here, above a sea of white cosmos 'Versailles', cleome and gypsophila, a hydroponics system was used to grow a potager in its nutrient-rich water. I thought at once of cliff-top houses, where windswept decks could be put to use for growing salads, tomatoes, peppers and aubergines, the staples of summer seaside living.

At a recent exhibition a massive piece of glass was made into a table. Glass bowls were let into the centre of it, each planted with a small selection of potager staples. Following a similar theme, British innovator Terence Conran created a rooftop potager, a silver and white design of square, shiny, metal tins crammed with vegetables and surrounded by moving water beside a bountiful refectory table.

Below: Golden pumpkins represented the rising and setting sun.

Opposite: Silvered olive oil drums surrounded by a sea of water grew all the ingredients for gazpacho soup – tomatoes, peppers, garlic and basil.

Below: Entitled 'O de Fleurs', this highly romantic potager was a garden to feed the senses; cool water trickled down the terracotta pipes, and rose petals floated in basins above aromatic herbs.

Top right: An idea for a roof top potager, with flowers, vegetables and herbs growing in containers of different heights and sizes.

Bottom right: Disused oil drum lids used to pave an urban potager.

Opposite: Woven garden supports placed to train creepers into imaginative green shapes.

# CHAPTER 7
## PLANNING A JARDIN POTAGER

# CHOOSING A SITE

If it is to be practical, the potager garden should be as close as possible to the kitchen door. Not only is it convenient for instant harvesting, but there are also the sensual delights of aromatic herbs and crisp growing vegetables nearby. At West Green House, my home in Britain, this was not possible. The existing layout of the garden meant that the potager had to be quite a distance from the house, so my immediate needs in the kitchen are met by plants in pots and a jumbled strip of lettuces, herbs and pansies planted by the back door. A potager created in a group of pots can be a captivating solution, but plants dry out more quickly and watering is a consideration. If the potager is to be purely decorative, you can put it where you wish, but wouldn't it look appealing as the foreground to the view from a dining room window?

There are no rules about how large or small a potager should be – the decision is all yours. Be sure to make it a manageable size though, and base your calculations on the help available to you. Remember, a potager is much more demanding than a simple row of shrubs surrounding the weekly argument, the mown lawn. To grow well, vegetables must be fed, weeded and watered. Herbs need to be trimmed and tied back, and fruit trees require pruning.

Ideally, the site should be flat and designed to drain quickly. I have found that even the slightest slope can cause difficulties. Water can collect against a boarded and hedged bed edge, or a solid, enclosing wall. Standing water causes roots to rot, endangering trees or hedges, which are the bones of the garden, as well as flooding the annual crops. Budget to level the area, it is essential.

Potagers were originally enclosed to keep out a hostile world. Today, enclosure is still to be desired, as walls and hedges can frame a design and break howling winds, protecting the new growth of leaf and fruit. In cooler climates they also trap warmth. Bricks warmed by the sun are especially kind to espaliered trees.

In warm climates, walls can cause problems. When I built my first potager at Burrumbuttock, New South Wales, I enclosed it in 1.8m (6ft) sand-rendered brick walls, inserting Victorian 'iron lace' as openings. Delightful in winter and early spring, it captured and held the summer heat, which was reflected once again by the hot paving stones. A cooling basin or pool of water in the Arab tradition would have moistened the air and helped my poor plants to survive, but I was still learning.

Circulating air helps to keep a garden healthy, so think carefully before building a wall. Warm, moist air can also be captured by trees or hedges. Thick hedges of *Cupressus torulosa* surround Kennerton Green's rose garden, ensuring that fungal diseases are thriving there by mid-summer.

Walls made from fruit trees allow air to move more freely than a solid wall would do. At le Prieuré Notre Dame d'Orsan, in central France, thick walls of plums completely conceal vegetables, flowers and herbs, while at Kennerton Green the 1.8m (6ft) high cords of apples allow humid air to circulate and give protection from strong winds.

Roses and apple trees have been allowed to form an impenetrable fence around the potager at Golden Point in Victoria, Australia, providing colour from both flower and fruit. This is a perfect way to cover an ordinary, country fence – as our medieval ancestors knew – and an excellent modern way to provide nearly rabbit and deer proof fencing.

Fences made from woven materials, such as wattle or hazel, bound tea tree or brush, and wooden trellis give pleasing texture, but they are not always long lasting. At Dangar Island, north of Sydney, my tea-tree fence lasted around five years in humid conditions, and the hazel woven fences at West Green have a similar lifespan before they rot at ground level. Quality trellis will last, but the garden centres' cheap and cheerful range is only for short-lived structures, providing useful support for annual vines and creepers.

Previous page: A potager needs to be easily maintained and the plants require a well drained soil, so a level space is ideal.

Opposite: The pathway leading from the cooling shade invites an inspection of the McCauslands' potager, which is enclosed to restrain four-legged predators. This potager is large enough to allow the plants to grow without fear of competition from encroaching roots and blanketing shade.

Left: Large stone walls protect plants and provide foundations for trellised grapes.

Above: Visitors enter the potager at Kennerton Green through a sturdy lychgate, designed as a sheltered spot for enjoying the garden.

# MAKING AN ENTRANCE

Enclosed potagers can become secret gardens. Often, the gate leading into the garden will be an important feature, suggesting the style or design of the garden beyond. At Kennerton Green I made a lychgate, its design copied from the one at the local church. It has a pitched slate roof and wooden benches on either side, to rest and retreat from sun and rain.

The garden at Dangar Island, Australia, was entered through a carved Balinese door let into a tea-tree hedge beneath an Oriental inspired portico of filigree, terracotta Balinese tiles placed along the pitch of tea-tree thatch. Another entrance way that I designed had a pitched roof completely smothered with hot pink *Rosa* 'Dorothy Perkins,' a prolific climber with small flowers.

One day I would like to make an entrance way with a gable covered with house leeks, those small, rosette-like succulents, or with a joining line of thatch held in place by bearded irises, a French country tradition said to deter the evil one.

So many American potagers were entered through freshly painted white picket gates, homely, charming and so inviting. Garden centres and hardware stores sell a wide variety of gates in diverse materials and finishes, and they can be an excellent starting point for making a decision.

Other gardens have no gates or doors, with just carved posts used to mark the entrance. I was captivated by a wooden owl used to mark the entrance of a potager in New York State. The choices are endless, the only true limits being those of the gardener's own imagination.

# PREPARING THE SITE

Spray or dig the site to eradicate all weeds. Wait for the germination of any surviving weed seeds and spray or dig again. This is vital as the garden will never again be as empty as it is now, and nothing is more labour intensive than chasing the roots of couch grass or ground elder among the roots of small hedges that border beds. Layers of paper or straw will strangle weeds in beds, but are not as effective at keeping the edges of beds weed-free.

Dense weed matting that denies light and moisture to unwanted grasses can be very effective, although not a beautiful sight. I suffered it for a whole summer as a last ditch solution, preferring not to use any chemicals if at all possible.

Herbs, fruit, vegetables and flowers are very hungry, so top dressing is an annual event. The new garden should be well mulched with compost or old manure. It is even better to dig it in, but I find digging too hard now, and I must trust to the worms, the rain and the tiller to send the goodness down.

If your soil is really poor or covered with clay from old foundations or builders' rubble, it is best to have it taken away, replacing it with good soil purchased from a reliable merchant.

# PLANNING THE LAYOUT

Now that the site is enclosed, level and weed free, it has become the perfect drawing board and the time has come to plan a layout. My own gardens were agonised over and redrawn endlessly. Finally, with the design finalised, I would go to the site with a well-bribed accomplice. We mapped out the beds with measuring tape, string and pegs, and then left it well alone. I would return again and again, reviewing the layout over the brim of a morning coffee or an evening glass of wine, for once any hard landscaping is done it is expensive and exasperating to make alterations.

The design process started for me with doodles on the back of an envelope, playing with geometric shapes. Once I had devised a pattern that pleased me, it was transferred to a generously sized piece of graph paper. I then took a step back to ensure that the design was practical, passing my plan on to a knowledgeable gardener and asking him or her for a critique. Next, measure the site carefully and ensure that the design is not too large or complicated, as it is better to err on the side of simplicity.

Above: In one part of the West Green House potager an entirely new potager is set out each spring. Here temporary sand paths and structures made from stakes tell a story through plant patterns. In the summer of 2000 our story was a central European cottage plot with a house made of beans.

Below: Geometric layouts tend to work best for potagers large or small, whether circular, square or rectangular.

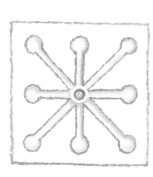
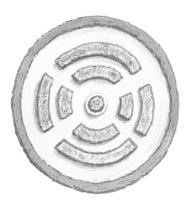

# MAKING PATHS

Now, having pegged out the layout on the ground, it is time to make the potager a reality. Paths are one of the most important aspects of the design, for this is a garden that never goes to sleep, and as an all-season affair, it must be accessible in every weather.

Ensure that the paths are wide enough to push a barrow along, but remember, paths that are too wide will make the pattern of the potager look sparse. On the other hand, rampant summer plantings can quickly colonise tiny paths, making maintenance and harvesting troublesome. Personally, I like paths to be around 1.2m (4ft) wide. I also like my main access paths to be larger than auxiliary ones.

Paths can be of mown grass, fine gravel, bricks, timber slats, flat stones, paving slabs, plain or decorated concrete. Pebbles or cobbles look wonderful but will unbalance an overloaded barrow.

Gravel, like bricks, allows rain to drain quickly. Choose a fine-textured stone, spread evenly and not too generously so that the barrow travels easily across it. Railway sleepers set in sand are another option, and they are very strong. Wooden slats keep the feet dry but they can become slippery and their lifespan, even if they are set in sand and treated against infestation, is only about a decade.

Mown grass is the cheapest option for a path. It is cool and inviting on a summer's day, although it can turn to mud in wet weather if is not well drained. It will also tend to gradually disappear over a period of time, as the edges eat their way a little more into the path each time they are straightened. If a grass path is planned, measure its width carefully so that it is compatible with the width of your mower's blade.

Paths are the bones of the garden, holding the design together and creating the character of the potager. A traditional potager is an intricate design, so an overly ornamented pathway can be confusing and unnecessary. However, at key points a design of coloured tiles or a change of paving design can be arresting. Above all, a path must be a safe and easy place to walk, enhancing your potager's appearance and encouraging visitors to explore further.

Left: My two favourite surfaces for paths, bricks (above) and gravel (below), although with constant raking gravel does disappear and needs to be topped up; a brick path is more expensive to build but is generally good forever.

# MAKING THE BEDS

Beds traditionally must be large enough to be enclosed by a low hedge, or perhaps a taller edging made from a vine or an espaliered tree, while still leaving room for a selection of flowers, vegetables or herbs.

Beds in a grid pattern can be tilled from four sides. I believe that the width of the bed should correspond to the reach of my hoe. At planting time, I leave spaces that will allow me to walk on the bed during harvesting, for surface roots do not appreciate being trampled on.

People tend to choose whatever is close at hand to make borders for their potager beds. Pine cones and seashells are two very appealing options. Scallop shells can be simply pushed into the ground by the flat edge, but beware, they are brittle, so a nearby beach is essential.

Beds can be edged in any way you please. Treated timbers, bricks, decorative terracotta tiles, hooped wire, rocks, shells or woven saplings are all options on an endless list. I like to use a solid edge of brick that soon supports moss and mellows comfortably, as terracotta will too. There are some splendid terracotta edging tiles available, although I always worry that a dropped tool could chip or crack them.

Micro-climates develop among plants, so moisture and air need to circulate and not be captured between too closely encircling hedges, which will cause rot or mildew.

Below left: The long narrow beds at St Jean de Beauregarde allow for easy maintenance and harvesting from both sides.

Below right: The wide beds have different edges, with new box cuttings on one side and a wide band of parsley on the other.

Following page: Espaliered apple trees in palmette style and pyramids of dense green *Cupressus* bring height and balance to the Mediterranean potager at Château Joanis in Provence.

# CHOOSING TREES

Potagers are like tabletops with tall objects placed on them for interest. The flat beds call out for the height of fruit trees trained or pruned into shapes. For potagers are productive gardens where plants require maximum sunlight to mature and ripen, and too many branching trees casting shade will negate its function. Pears, like apples, will respond to training. In warmer climates, oranges and grapefruits can be trained along wires and will clip into large standard balls or can be cut into square shapes. Bay trees can be clipped too, into balls or cones. By twisting the growing trunk around a solid stick a twisted stem can be achieved. Kennerton Green has eighty-one bay trees planted this way to make a formal grid.

Lemons, limes, kumquats, pomegranates and olives can add height to large tubs, but can only be considered for warmer climates. Grey artichokes in terracotta pots create their own architecture in an English summer garden, but lines of flowering trees cut into topiary balls on elegant stems create permanent patterns of great excitement.

In hot, dry climates, consider the *Pittosporum tobira* or *Lantana camara,* the scented mock orange with flowers of many colours, which becomes a noxious weed in humid coastal areas. *Eucalyptus perriniana*, the blue-purple spinning gum, or *Callistemon citrinus*, the scarlet bottlebrush, colourful Australian natives, but hardiest of all is *Nerium oleander* cut into tough pompom trees that tolerate even the most neglectful gardener.

In humid gardens, *Gardenia jasminoides* has the shiniest dark green leaves below white flowers of the most divine scent. Hawaiian hibiscus has saucer flowers of sunset colours that seem to belong in a travel poster. In Sydney gardens I have spied outrageous, purple *Lasiandra macrantha* clashing above a floor of forming orange pumpkins, outstanding balls of colour on standard stems .

As well as box, holly and yew, cool temperate gardens can be dressed with weigela. At West Green ours is called 'Ruby', a vibrant coloured bush cut as a spring mop head. Compact, evergreen, *Viburnum tinus* with pink to white flowers in winter, tough cotoneaster with bright red berries and *Syringa persica*, with fragrant, tidy, lilac flowers in early May, line the paths as round-head sentinels.

Every where I go I plant standard lavenders and rosemarys. In the fruit cages of West Green House are red, white and black currants and standard mop head gooseberries, with welcome strawberries at their feet. Raspberries train up the central pole and pots of huckleberries arrive to add dark autumn colour to this protected berry forest.

Columnar cypressus grow naturally into formal fingers and will tolerate seasonal climbers. They will respond to shaping or bending into arches and can even be trained around tall sticks to become giant screws, often with an unlikely knob or curl on top if the gardener is so minded.

I like to include a fig tree, both for its purple-brown fruit and the wonderful story in Genesis 3: 'As soon as they had eaten it, they were given the understanding and realised that they were naked; so they sewed the fig leaves together and covered themselves.' Fig trees respond well to espaliering and will line fences or walls, covering their nakedness too with their fine, wide leaves as the summer approaches. Browse in the decorative garden shops to find stylish

# SUPPORTS AND STRUCTURES

supports for your plants, or make tripods for tomatoes and other climbers from garden stakes, bamboo or twigs from the woods tied together to form the simplest of supports. The height that they give is remarkably effective when supporting standard beans, peas, sweet peas and nasturtiums. Later in the season they will be smothered with morning glories (*Ipomoea versicolor*) trumpets of blue streaked with purple, or the cardinal-red *Ipomoea* x *multifida*.

Tunnels and arches can be woven from an assortment of annual plants. Walk beneath the orange and gold vegetable ornaments of gourds, courgettes, beans, sunflowers and nasturtiums, all loomed together. This is time consuming to achieve but very rewarding. My arches are set in pairs at Mittagong in Australia. Two of them support white grapes and two dark passion fruit. At West Green the golden crab apple carries the gold of the summer climbing rose, 'Marigold' across the arches.

Arches, trellises and tripods provide the drama of verticle height and allow for additional colour to be introduced; I have just painted benches in two different shades of lavender to look strong against eucalyptus green. Boldly coloured structures can also screen urban gardens or add interest to dull and underplanted patches. Permanent plantings require host structures that are well made and enduring. At West Green House roses eventually strangled enchanting wooden arbours, pieces of which were carried away by gnarled and rampant growth. Wrought iron or steel mesh structures will prevent later anguish and hold the goliaths of the garden world quite happily.

# SEATS AND ARBOURS

Seats and arbours made from woven willow and covered in new green leaves bring inspiration in springtime. All seats are tremendously important, not just to sit and dream on, but for placing tools, sorting plants and cleaning vegetables. Herbs such as thyme and camomile can be planted in the cracks of stone benches, so that the air is filled with their scent when they are crushed.

Seats can be as grand or simple as the potager requires. Barrow-style seats are fun as they can be wheeled around the garden to follow the sun. The most glorious seats I've seen are made by the Chatsworth Carpenters in Britain – I just stand and wish!

# BIRDS AND WATER FEATURES

The monks of the Middle Ages must have known both how important and how tiring watering could be. A pond or a canal was always made near to the potager, or sometimes the garden was sited near to a well.

For a small potager in a temperate climate a tap and watering can will do. Gardens in Australia or in a Mediterranean climate, however, will need an irrigation system if annual vegetables, flowers, herbs and fruit trees are to survive and be productive. I favour overhead sprays attached to a timer. Ideally, there should also be water to supply a central pond or fountain, the symbol of life in the garden.

Water features, fountains, ponds and irrigation canals, whether simple or decorative, add sparkle and freshness to the potager. They can be filled with sacred Koi carp, goldfish or waterlilies, or made into a watercress garden. We believe that the ancestor of the potager was the paradise or oasis garden, its grids dissected by canals of flowing water to cool a Middle Eastern courtyard and bring refreshment to plants and people.

I have just designed an oblong courtyard that is completely dissected by open pipes of water. They form squares that are broken by two large, square ponds. Leading away from this strict geometry are parallel lines of espaliered pomegranate and pear, rows of figs and interlocking squares of dwarf pear varieties made into two mazes. It looks sharp and modern, but the concept was lifted from Mogul miniature paintings.

The pictures in Medieval manuscripts show gardens with bees, chickens, ducks, peacocks and birds. The

peacocks that once strutted around my Mittagong garden in Australia are now in a large cage to foil the foxes. A chicken run forms the other side of my Australian potager, but the fantail pigeons are banished. They are nothing but wicked white purity, having wiped out new seedlings and pecked holes in large leaves. Decorative dovecotes are hard to resist, but ornamental birdcages filled with vibrant coloured birds replace the vandals very well.

The lines of beehives depicted in Medieval manuscripts are very attractive, and the sound of bees is a joyful thing. Never forget, however, that they do swarm. Ducks are another potential inhabitant for the potager. Although they are effective as snail vacuum cleaners, they are muck-making machines, too.

Opposite, clockwise from top left: Tall sticks cut from the forest are magical supports for annual climbing plants at le Prieuré Notre Dame d'Orsan; painted garden supports, seats and arbours can change the garden's mood each time they are painted; the apple tree from which eve plucked the apple shelters visitors at the centre of the maze at le Prieuré Notre Dame d'Orsan.

Above: The strutting, fluffy and huffing off a collection of prize Peking chickens add a joyous note to the garden at West Green House.

# PLANS FOR AN URBAN POTAGER

Opposite, clockwise from top: A hydroponic potager placed on timber decking allows herbs, lettuce, aubergines and tomatoes to grow superbly; picture book tomatoes trained up a cone-shaped support in a rooftop garden; the sunflower is an expected inhabitant of any potager, but the miniature variety 'Toy Box' is small enough for any city garden.

Following page, left to right: At Kennerton Green chives edge and divide groups of plants; Red Mountain Spinach is a must-have plant, as its foliage complements any colour backing, from mauves to oranges, reds and yellows.

The long, oblong back yards of suburbia worldwide are the ideal territory for a potager. They offer the right dimensions for the historic quadrant, and the meagre space, which can be so dreary and barren, can become a stage. It is a space of moving shadows surrounded by walls and fences and is the ideal setting for exhilarating colours, derived not only from vegetables, flowers and fruit, but also from the physical architecture of the garden.

I would abandon precise timber and white trellis in this setting, along with antique or rusty artefacts and even the traditional, evergreen hedge. My walls would be espaliered with fruit trees, their branches on wires standing proud of their wooden supports. This would allow me to paint the timber a brilliant red behind the green apples, green behind the red fruit and marigold for the pears.

My purple 'Cosse Violette' beans would be framed in tripods of royal blue and violet, and the cream and red bean Barlotto 'Tongues of Fire' would be attached to rich red and yellow supports. The names of my seeds would be written on primary coloured squares nailed to stakes in the ground. Terracotta would be replaced with glazed pots of shiny cobalt blues, grass greens and ruby reds.

Pathways would be made from ethnic tiles of fearsome designs and colours to banish concrete-grey. The decorous urn or antique sculpture at the centre of the garden would be replaced by a topiary monster or a big bird made from a rose woven around a frame. These will grow within five years – or you could save time and buy one ready made. Water could take the form of a pond or fountain of coloured glass lit from beneath to create a glowing oasis.

Wigwams of hazel for supporting beans or tomatoes can be tied together with colourful ropes. Bright orange 'Jack o'Lantern' pumpkins can be trained up arches of wide netting, creating burning suns in the sky. In autumn, these could be picked and placed on the cleared earth in parade ground patterns, extending the colour season in the garden.

Garden designer Sarah Raven has lit corners of her garden with poles inspired by Venetian gondolier moorings. They are painted in rich colours and ornamented with stripes of gold. American glass artist Dale Chihaly created a forest of fire red glass poles. Exhibited in Australia, they captured every prism of light and glowed with an inner energy. He played the same games with a small wooden dinghy filled with glass balls, which he floated on a pond. I was so entranced by this concept that I went so far as to ring his agent. The following morning I went out to my own pond where my dingy is anchored. Unfortunately, the ducks had nested there over night, putting paid to my plans. It was a sensational idea while it lasted!

When you are choosing flowers, throw caution to the winds. In early spring, *Cirsium rivulare* 'Atropurpureum,' a tall, magenta thistle, amongst fronds of the nearly white flowers and black stems of cow parsley, *Anthriscus sylvestris* 'Ravenswing.' Create late season height with tall dahlias, using colours too outspoken for a considered border. Be dashing and try large, bold, purple, red and white tipped 'Tartan'. It could carry through the purple section of the garden after the sweet peas had been removed. Under the spiky, cardinal-red cactus dahlia 'Rotterdam', I'd bank the yellow centred daisies of *Aster dumosus* 'Anneke', bright red and flowering happily into autumn. The yellow and orange vegetables would welcome the yellow and orange striped rose *Rosa* 'Oranges and Lemons', a Floribunda, or *R.* 'Tequila Sunrise', another hybrid whose red buds turn to yellow edged in red. Plant it with *Zinnia* 'Old Mexico', which is a red-orange tipped with yellow. The Mexican, orange-gold *cosmos* 'Sunrise and Sunset', not well known but beginning to appear in many catalogues, could be a friend for the oval, yellow tomato 'Bavaria Legs'.

We are surrounded by a minimalist world of greys and blacks, so let our flowery vegetable gardens rejoice in colour. The jewelled tones of a Medieval manuscript can transform a plot into our own vision of paradise.

# EDGING PLANTS

### Box

*(Buxus)* Evergreen shrub or tree

Closely-clipped box still makes the neatest edges. It is tolerant of heat and humidity, flourishing even in extreme climates. For a low hedge, choose a smaller leaved variety, otherwise every leaf looks as if it has been chopped in half.

Box looks cool and fresh even on the hottest days. It forms a green tracery pattern in gardens when all else is dormant and becomes pure magic when covered in snow.

Box, for most of us, is nearly trouble free and responds happily to regular clipping. Be sure to put small plants into weed-free soil, water in hot weather and feed annually.

English gardeners need to consult a good nurseryman to ensure their plant is not prone to box disease.

### Chives

*(Allium schoenoprasum)* Perennial

The fine grey spikes of chives make the easiest and cheapest edging plants. They quickly form a thick row, covered with round, mauve, clover flowers before the plants become straggly and need a crew cut. Good gardeners plant wide bands of chives and rotate their growth. They cut some to the ground, allow others to reach mid-height, and leave a final line to flower. This ensures that one section is in colourful flower throughout the growing season.

### Parsley

*(Petroselinum crispum)* Annual

Curly parsley in rich green banks makes a hem of lace around a potager, but this only happens when it is grown in fertile and well-watered soil. If you can grow it well, nothing is more fresh, vibrant and decorative as an edging. Parsley's growing season ends when hard frost appears.

### Rosemary

*(Rosmarinus officinalis)* Woody shrub

Rosemary tolerates long summers, heat and dryness, but needs protection in colder climates. It clips into the neat hedges with fine, aromatic foliage and blue flowers in spring. There are also forms with small white and pink blooms. Rosemary strikes easily from small cuttings to form a hedge. Plant out in rows about 30cm (12in) apart.

### Rue

*(Ruta graveolens)* Perennial

The rue 'Jackman's Blue', kept clipped into clumps of aqua blue, can make a soft, fluid edge to a bed. Rue needs sun to maintain its blue colouring, but behaves well in any soil, although trimming is a must to prevent height and woodiness.

# PERSONAL
# PLANT CHOICES

# PLANTS TO GIVE HEIGHT

VEGETABLES AND HERBS

### Angelica

*(Angelica archangelica)* Biennial

Tall, sturdy stems hold enormous round heads of pale green above fronds of ferny leaves. *Angelica gigas* has deep burgundy umbels atop branches of the same colour measuring over 1m (3ft) tall . It is a late-summer goliath to take over from the pinnacles of black hollyhocks (*Alcea rosea*) for soaring height.

### Amaranthus

*(Amaranthus gangeticus*, Elephants Head) Annual

Giant and tough enough to withstand altitude, cold and heat, it's great purple heads of seeds are sensational garden architecture, weird and wonderful in late summer. Grown originally by ancient, central American tribes for grain, its many other varieties today provide plumes, tassels and extraordinarily shaped plants for garden excitement.

### Sweetcorn

*(Zea mays)* Annual

Sweetcorn is planted once the ground is warm, shooting up to over 1.2m (4ft) with cobs of yellow, white, gold, or purple, red, blue and bicoloured. I love 'Bloody Butcher', an American heirloom variety with blood-red kernels and wine-red husks that can shoot up to 3 m (10 ft) high! 'Red Stalker' has 8 ft red and purple stalks, which are often cut and used for temporary garden hedges.

### Globe artichokes

*(Cynara scolymus)* Annual

Tall and graceful, these plants are pure aristocrats, , bearing round grey or blue flower buds. If they are not harvested, the flowers turn into large, lavender-blue thistles. Graceful as specimens in pots, they make stately additions to a mixed border, enjoying a fertile soil. They will happily tolerate spells of dry weather. Their growing cycle concludes towards the end of summer, but they will reshoot after being cut back, regaining their silver-grey leaves in warmer autumn gardens.

### Orach or Red Mountain Spinach

*(Atriplex hortensis)* Annual

Tall, often growing to 1.5m (5ft), this plant has ruby like, brown- burgundy leaves, which glow red-purple in the afternoon sun. It is a hardy, self-seeding plant, generally grown for its foliage, but the new leaves also have excellent flavour. It likes the sun but tolerates some shade. It will need watering during extra-dry, hot spells. Mix with the tall red dahlias 'Arabian Knight' for a devastating and wonderful wall of ruby.

## Dahlias

*(Dahlia)* Tuberous perennial

My conversion from mild acceptance to admiration of dahlias came after my visit to Kasteel Hex in Belgium, where they were planted as a Berlin Wall of flowers to protect the vegetables from the free world. 'Marie Schnugg' is an excellent, single red, and 'David Howard' has purple leaves around orange flowers that balance the golds, oranges and mahogany of rudbeckia planted alongside, echoing the colours of late-summer vegetables. Tall varieties of dahlias do need staking. Dahlia tubers should be lifted and stored for winter in a dry space away from pests.

## Rose

*(Rosa)* Perennial shrub

A familiar legend has it that the monks placed a rose in each garden plot, thus honouring the Virgin and her place in the mysticism of the Medieval church, and so I must give them a place in the *jardin potager*.

Extra tall, standard roses of a repeating variety can bring 1.5m (5ft) of romance to a potager during the summer months. I prefer strong coloured roses against the bright green of the vegetables; especially the sunset tones that reflect the hues of autumn abundance. Roses are greedy, quite thirsty and sun loving, so they rejoice in a well-mulched vegetable garden. They can be used to edge borders. I have used the blood-red *Rosa* 'Marlene', a strong, continuously flowering bush-rose just over 30cm (1ft ) tall for a gash of red fencing.

## Sweet Pea

*(Lathyrus odoratus)* Annual

A climber, the sweet pea can add vital colour and perfume if it is grown among marrows and sunflowers over the framework of a tunnel. Grown separately on a tripod, sweet peas add both height and a hint of nostalgia to the potager. They love full sun, becoming sulky and refusing to grow during wet years. Old varieties will self-seed, but most modern climbers must be sown annually.

One of the best garden effects I have achieved was to grow a royal-blue sweet pea through the two-toned purple flower of the Dutch, purple-podded pea 'Capucyner', so that it smothered a tripod.

## Sunflower

*(Helianthus annus)* Annual

Try a teddy-bear type, 'Giant Sungold' that has cheerful discs and fully double flowers growing to 2m (6ft). It is excellent as a backdrop, for encircling a secret garden or grown side by side to make a palisade.

## Verbascum olympicum

Semi-evergreen biennial

White, woolly leaves and 2m (6ft) stems clothed with bright yellow flowers right to their very top. They love sun and will thrive in a neglected corner, or plant them in a gravel path beside a coloured bench for sheer impact.

Trees in the *jardin potager* are generally pruned, trained or shaped to maximise production and to limit the amount of shade that they throw.

Opposite and above: Dahlias in two of Europe's most admired potagers, Kasteel Hex opposite, emphasising the height of corn, and St Jean de Beauregarde above.

Top: Miniature sunflowers alongside scarlet red sweetpeas about to climb an orange, timber tripod in my garden, 2001.

# FRUIT TREES

## Apples and Pears

*(Malus and Pyrus)*

So enamoured am I with these trees that I once bought a block of land just to own an old pear tree that stood there. Apple and pear trees give so much: clouds of unsurpassed spring blossom, thick green leaves, sweet fruit to eat and juice to drink. They will happily allow us to twist them into fanciful, espaliered shapes, creating dividing walls or growing tunnels. The single, columnar 'Ballerina' shapes bear both apple and crab apple varieties and dwarf varieties of pears make exceptional pot plants. For those of us who love to weave biblical studies into our potagers, the symbolism of the offered apple makes it essential.

Grafted to appropriate rootstock, apples will grow from northern Europe to the Mediterranean. Pears like it slightly warmer, they flower freely trained to a chimneystack in my cooler garden, but they also grow well in the sub-tropical regions north of Sydney.

Above: The colour of the turning grape vine opposite and this deep red pear made one of the most arresting colour combinations in the old potager at St Jean de Beauregarde.

Right: The hexagonal fruit cages at West Green House protect berry fruits, and here, beside scarlet clusters of red currents, the gooseberries, white currents and raspberries thrive in safety above a carpeting of strawberries.

## Bay Tree

*(Laurus nobilis)*

Rubbing the strong, deep green, spicey smelling, oval leaves of the bay, it is easy to understand why the victors of the Ancient world were crowned with wreaths of laurel.

Clipped into cones or mop heads, used as features in tubs, this evergreen tree always looks crisp, clean and green. A Mediterranean plant, it copes with heat and dust, but in Britain I've lost young trees to frost.

## Kumquat

*(Fortunella)*

For those of us who live where frosts are light and the days are warm, these are small, neat trees with ever-polished leaves, studded with ping pong balls of pure orange. Delightful in pots for lining paths, they always look perfect whatever the season.

Their small, bitter fruit is used in jams and put down smothered in brandy for future liqueurs. 'Nagami', with its oval fruit, and 'Marumi', a perfect sphere, are both favoured by Australian gardeners.

Kumquats detest heavy soil where drainage is poor. They would rather put up with some neglect, waiting for a good feed of organic fertiliser and a drink once a week than die from waterlogged feet.

## Medlar

*(Mespilus)*

These are small trees covered with handsome leaves held in dense bunches. They are tolerant of frost and drought, growing happily in a lawn or as a hedge. Medlar trees rarely need pruning, as they grow so slowly. In spring they are centred with solitary, creamy-white, star-shaped flowers. Their calyx forms the punched-in-nose frill of the deep brown, round, autumn fruit which is the size of a golf ball. I've never eaten the spicy fruits, but I love to display them with the red, gold and bronze autumn leaves in a vase.

## Olives

*(Olea europaea)*

For gardens in Mediterranean or lightly frosted, temperate climates the olive tree has left the hills and orchards to become a fashion statement. Planted in lush, tended lawns, they could die from too much attention. Olives like it tough, reflecting their native habitat. They even survive in neglected tubs at the Sydney Opera House, battered by endless wind and sea spray, home to seagulls and fast food wrappers.

White flowers cover the dark grey leaves, silvered beneath in spring and followed by green or black fruit in summer. They are trees that rarely need pruning. I've had success in Australia with 'Sievillano' and 'Kerdale' varieties.

Olives symbolise peace, hope and a new life. A passage in Genesis reads: 'He [Noah] waited another seven days and sent out the dove again. It returned to him in the evening with a fresh olive leaf in its beak.'

Above: The tiny pear is captured in a bottle to commence its new career as a perfect fruit surrounded by delicious liqueur.

# PLANTS NEEDING SUPPORT

**Beans**

*(Phaseolus vulgaris)*

The variety of beans available seems to grow annually and I am always tempted to try out too many. Beans are reliable, easy to grow and ego boosting for the new gardener. They can be draped over tripods or trellises, where they loom high above the ground, huge and verdant, convincing everyone who sees them that you are an exceptional gardener.

I like red and pink-white flowers of the runner bean 'Painted Lady', with a rich beany taste, and also the red-splashed shelling bean Borlotto 'Tongues of Fire 2', steamed and tossed with oil and herbs. Bellissimo!

Underplant beans with radishes as they help to deter insects, and I am assured they improve the flavour of the beans too. Beans enrich the soil and are invaluable to the health of a productive potager.

**Chilean Glory Vine**

*(Eccremocarpus scaber)* Evergreen sub-shrub

By early August the trailing plants engulf the garden, and none is so flamboyant as the Chilean glory vine, with tubular bells in carmine, rose, apricot, orange and scarlet hanging from deep purple- brown stems. Flowering throughout these warm days, it prefers well-drained soils that are rich and moist. It is equally happy in potagers in Northamptonshire, in Britain, and Delaware, USA. In both gardens it makes the maximum vertical display, casting dappled shade on the garden below.

**Climbing Nasturtiums**

*(Tropaeolum majus)* Annual

You must be passionate about nasturtiums before you let them into your garden, for once you have planted them they self-seed forever.

Spicy, with the hint of watercress, their brilliant faces are among the best-known edible flowers, capable of lifting a humble salad to great culinary heights.

I have never had problems growing nasturtiums, but I despair of controlling them. Today they are available world wide in cream, butter, scarlet and mahogany shades, with leaves that are mottled or have a blue-green sheen to them. The new varieties of this cottage-garden plant are horticultural years away from the usual orange and yellow thugs.

**Morning Glory**

*(Ipomoea)* Annual

In the warm air of Sydney, the common morning glory (*Ipomoea purpurea*) with its indigo flowers engulfs entire gardens, every flower smiling at you to welcome the day. Rampant, beautiful pests, taunting you to be mean enough to cut them back, for they pose a self-seeding dilemma.

In other warm climates these plants feature as pure white moonflowers (*Ipomoea alba*), unfurling at sunset to perfume the air, or the crimson cardinal climber (*Ipomoea x multifida*), with bright red flowers climbing to the spires of hospitable supports.

## Passionfruit

(*Passiflora edulis*) Evergreen/Semi-evergreen climber

When people ask me what I miss when gardening in an English garden I know there are only two plants I pine for – the lemon tree and the passionfruit vine. Passionfruits will grow in the warmer areas of the cool temperate zone, where frosts are mild, in light soils. The prolific vines reach for the sun, romping up pagodas and arbours, clinging to whatever is within their reach. Passionfruit enjoy a dose of sulphate of ammonia, but mine survive on a good mulch each autumn, giving abundant crops of dark purple fruit in February and March in Australia.

*Passiflora*, the passion flower, will grow in cool conservatories. Nothing is more spectacular than *P. antiquiensis*, its astonishing flower reminding me of a red and purple spider.

# VEGETABLES TO EXTEND THE SEASON: WINTER

## Brussels Sprouts

*(Brassica Oleracea* Capitata Group*)* Annual

I have always believed that Brussels sprouts merit a place in the front garden. With their curious appearance – tall stems nobbled with bunions and crowned by a top-knot of leaves – they are valiant decorations during the barest season.

Plant in early summer, or three or four months before the crop is required for a scrumptious winter treat. Rural sages say that they taste best after a good frost.

I like to grow both the green and purple varieties of sprouts, simply for their colour. 'Rubine' is a decorative red, as is Suttons' 'Falstaff', and American 'Igor' can tolerate a cold, wet autumn. Christmas dinner would be a non-event without mounds of these tiny green balls of leaf, crisp and nut flavoured, encircling the brown chestnuts.

## Cabbage

*(Brassica Oleracea* Gemmifera Group*)* Annual

Boarding school boiled cabbage turned me against these beautiful plants for many years, until one day I discovered that the wonderful purple leaves surrounded by bright pink zinnias in a glossy magazine were actually 'Red Drumhead' cabbages, and now I cannot imagine planting a garden without them.

One of the most beautiful cabbages is 'January King' with its red, blue and green leaves at their best from November to February. Plant out at least 30cm (12in) apart in summer in well-mulched earth, and remember to water them in their early stages.

Birds love young cabbage leaves and the white cabbage moth is an appalling nuisance, spoiling the decorative leaves with huge holes. Spray with a Pyrethethrum mix or try companion planting; orange marigolds planted near cabbages look so smart, even if you are not too sure about their effectiveness.

Previous page, from left: Delicious to eat and visually splendid 'Capucyner' purple podded peas grow equally well in my English and Australian gardens; for most of us the passion flower is a hot house wonder, but they can be seen trailing across garden fences in Sydney and points further north.

Left, from top: The multi-coloured stemmed chard has over wintered in pots in the garden at West Green House, providing stripes of colour on grey days, and then a matching foil for the *Viridi flora* tulips; the Red Drumhead Cabbage.

## Kale

*(Brassica Oleracea Acephalia Group)* Annual

Manly survivors against the toughest winters, handsome escorts to summer perennials and bright colour against crisp snow, these are the most handsome plants I know

With deep purple stems, 'Red Russian' grows up to 1m (3ft) tall. I have never eaten it but am told that it is delicious steamed with lemon and butter. 'Tuscan Black' kale, with its long, black-green, curly leaves, acts like black velvet, showing off all the gem-like garden colours in the summer, and becoming an elegant statement in winter. It is more delicious, I am told, as the temperature drops. Its stems can be chopped up for stir fries or put into stews and soups. Plant in late spring then stand back and watch your seedlings become garden collosuses.

## Leeks

*(Allium porrum)* Annual

Braised in soups or spiced as a salad, Leeks are a gourmet vegetable, and in the garden they are an artist's delight, with their wide, blue-grey, strappy leaves which produce a glorious flower next season, if not harvested.

'St Victor' with its purple-tinged, mid-winter leaves, and 'King Richard' which can withstand the heaviest frosts, to look fresh and neat by February, are popular varieties in Europe and America.

Leeks are extremely hardy and they grow well in poorer soils. They are planted in late spring for a winter harvest. Always part of a medieval potager, they were grown by monks as a substitute for garlic.

## Parsnips

*(Pastinaca sativa)* Annual

Mike Rendell, who gardens at West Green, frowns dreadfully if the parsnips are pulled up before they have been properly frosted, as this heightens their sugar content. We accuse him of hoarding them for parsnip wine!

These are one of the most uncomplaining vegetables, happy to grow from the tropics to zones where the garden freezes. Liking a well-drained soil, they are sown by drilling seed into prepared furrows, and they grow in situ, to be thinned out after the frilly tops appear. Parsnips need a full season to mature and are slow to germinate. Put a row of radishes beside the new seeds, as they germinate nearly instantly and make an excellent marker.

Above: In the last weeks of April we have a tulip festival at West Green House, and last season's Red Bor Kale provided a dramatic background for the flamboyant blooms of *Tulipa* 'Yomina' (lilac), 'Dreaming Maid' (pink) and 'Attlia' (purple).

# VEGETABLES FOR EARLY SPRING

### Broad Beans

(*Vicia faba*)

Two years ago I purchased a crimson flowered broad bean as a single specimen. I had been enchanted by its colour and pale grey leaf, but as I looked at it sitting beside me on the front seat of the car in solitary splendour, I decided that I was loopy to buy only one broad bean plant. To offset this extravagance we collected the seed and now they have become a brilliant exclamation mark in the early spring garden. The plant produces good bean pods, but perhaps the most readily available varieties are the white-flowered 'Early Long Read' and 'Saville'. They need space to grow and string on either side of them to keep them upright.

Broad beans enrich the soil by putting back nutrients. They like cool, temperate climates best, but will grow in Mediterranean zones. I find they attract all kinds of pests, and I paln to see if the poached egg plant (*Limnanthes douglasii*) or pot marigolds (*Calendula*) will help by enticing aphids and black fly to their upturned faces.

### Lambs lettuce/Corn salad

(*Valerianella*)

Sown in autumn to be the first green salad leaf of spring, lamb's lettuce is extremely pretty, its smooth oval leaves growing in rosettes. There are French and Italian varieties now available at the local garden centre. This is a green for cooler climates, as it bolts quickly when the temperature rises and quickly produces flowers.

### Rhubarb

(*Rheum rhaponticum*)

Safe and secure within a tall, terracotta forcing pot, hot pink stems of rhubarb with crinkled lemon leaves make the most incredible colour statement, and they can be ready for eating in January in the northern hemisphere.

Once the lid is removed in spring the huge leaves burst from their chimney pots making bold leaf structure in the garden. Terracotta forcing pots in lines transform a humble garden into a designer potager in an instant!

### Sea kale

(*Beta vulgaris*)

The dull, wand-like stems of sea kale are dusted on top with heads of cream-white flowers shooting up from crimped silver-grey leaves. The stems, blanched in the protected dark by a bucket or pot, are like evil creatures from another planet, pale and spooky to be cut and enjoyed as an early season delicacy.

### Rocket

(*Eruca*)

Have you read any smart restaurant menu without at least one mention of rocket? It is the international chef's favourite green: peppery sweet and ridiculously easy to grow. From earliest spring sow into tilled soil. It germinates in days and is often ready to cut within three weeks. Keep sowing regularly, as it bolts, runs to seed and looks scraggy – it is not a plant for a prominent place.

# AUTUMN

### Fennel

*(Foeniculum vulgare)*

In autumn, the fine, feathery leaves of fennel create a soft texture, catching any breeze and creating movement.

Grown for its layered, oval bulb, it is a marvellous salad vegetable, with an aniseed flavour and the texture and crunch of celery. For an autumn harvest, plant in summer in warmer climates and spring in temperate zones.

### Giant Red Mustard

Another plant that likes the cool weather with large, deep red-purple leaves. Even if the new, Dijon-mustard-flavoured leaves are not harvested, they look stunning beside the burnt coloured vegetables. Place seedlings 15cm (6in) apart to show off their beauty.

### Squash: Red Kuri

*Cururbita spp.*

Shaped like a flat-bottomed pear in the richest and most vivid orange, this is autumn colour at its zenith.

Red Kuri is an excellent cooking variety; with a flavour similar to that of chestnuts. Like all squash, its vine needs room to manoeuvre, producing four to five vegetables to a plant. Try training it along a waist-high ledge to show off its blazing nuggets.

### Gourds

*Cururbita Pepo Heirloom*

Gourds are grown simply because it is fun to see their wildly exotic shapes hanging from rampant vines. Their names conjure up astonishing images. I can never decide if 'Turks Turban' looks as if it should be on a pasha's head or served as an orange, green and white striped cottage loaf. 'Crown of Thorns' bears small globes with ten spikes in multi colours, and 'Yellow Warted' is covered with gruesome barnacles. The list goes on and on.

### Everlasting or Straw flowers

*(Helichrysum)*

No matter how high the mercury rises or how dry and dusty the autumn garden becomes, helichrysum , a native Australian plant, thrives and provides stiff, bright, daisy-shaped, autumn colour in the potager. It grows happily in average soil, demanding only modest amounts or water and enjoying regular harvesting and hot, hot sun.

Now available in separate colours, helichrysum is ideal for the potager stylist, especially its more petite forms that grow to only 25cm (10in) and are not so prone to wind destruction.

# BIBLIOGRAPHY

Blazey, Clive *The Australian Vegetable Garden*
Australia, New Holland, 1999

Brookes, John *Gardens of Paradise,* London,
Weidenfeld, 1987

Clevely, A.M. *The Integrated Garden*, London,
Barrie & Jenkins, 1988

Harvey, John *Medieval Gardens*, London, B. T.
Batsford, 1981

Hobhouse, Penelope *Plants in Garden History*,
London, Pavillion, 1992

Hemphill, Rosemary *Herbs for all Seasons*, rev.
ed., Australia, Angus Robertson, 1992

Jones, Louisa *French Country Gardens*, 2nd
ed., London, Thames and Hudson, 2000

Jones, Louisa *The Art of the French Vegetable
Garden*, USA, Artisan, 1995

Lansberg, Sylvia *The Medieval Garden*,
London, British Museum Press, 1998

Mawrey, Gillian *Villandry, The People, Not The
Potager*, London, Hortus, 1991

Pliny the Younger, *The Letters of the Younger
Pliny*, trans. B. Radice, Harmondsworth, 1967

Stewart, David C. *The Kitchen Garden*,
London, Robert Hale, 1984

Wilkinson, N. B. *Ei du Pont, Botaniste*,
Charlotesville, University of Virginia Press,
1972

Fazzar, Lindsay *Ancient Roman Gardens,*
Sutton Publishing, 1998

Leach, Helen *Cultivating Myths,* New Zealand,
Random House, 2000

# ADDRESSES

Diggers Garden Club
105 La Trobe Parade
Dromana
Victoria 3936 Australia
Tel: 0061359871877
Fax: 0061359814298

Kennerton Green
Bong Bong Road
Mittagong
NSW 2575 Australia
Tel. 0061248721719

The Potager/B&B
Golden Point
RSD181
Castlemaine
Victoria 3450 Australia
Tel: 0061354723714
Fax: 0061354724864
greatplacestostay.com.au/potager

Kasteel Hex
B 3870 Heers
Belgium
Tel 00411274 7341
Fax 0041 1274 4987
Email gardens@hex.be

The Old Rectory
Sudborough
Northamptonshire NN14 3BX
Tel 01832 733 247
Fax 01832 733832
Email jardann@aol.com

West Green House
Near Hartley Wintney
Hampshire RG27 8JB
Fax: 01252 844611

Château d'Opme
63540 Romagnat
France
Tel/Fax: 0033473875485

Château Val-Joannis
84120 Pertuis
France
Tel: 0033490792077
Fax: 0033490096952
Website: http://www.val-joanis.com
Email: info.visites@val-joanis.com

Château de Villandry
37510 VILLANDRY
FRANCE
Tel 0033247500209
Email: villandry@wanadoo.fr

les Jardins du Prieuré Notre Dame d'Orsan
18170 Maisonnais
Départementale 65 between Lioniéres and
Le Châtelet
25 km west of St. Amand de Montrond de
Berry
FRANCE
Tel. 0033248562750
Fax 0033248563964
Website: www.prieuredorsan.com

Bretton Garden
855 B&A Boulevard
Annapolis
Maryland 21146
Tel. 0014106476859

Hagley Museum and Garden
Route 141 (P.O. Box 3630)
Wilmington, DE  19807-0630
USA
Tel. 0013026582400
www.hagley.org

# INDEX

# ACKNOWLEDGEMENTS

Thanks to the many gardeners who allowed Clay Perry to photograph and who talked so long about their gardens to me.

In Australia, Mr Peter Brachen, Mrs Jane Evans, Mr Ian Huxley, my friend Mr Clive Blazey and my gardening team at Kennerton Green headed by David McKinley.

Thanks to Count d'Ursel and his staff at Kasteel Hex in Belgium.

In France, I thank the owners and gardeners of Villandry, St Jean de Beauregarde, Château d'Opme and my friends Cecile Chancel at Château Joanis, Sonia Lesot and Patrice Taravella at le Prieuré Notre Dame d'Orsan.

In the United States, Mr 'Nick' Du Pont and the Eleuthère Mills/Hagley Foundations, Mr and Mrs McCausland, Mrs Sluder and Mr Bob Ray.

In the United Kingdom, I spent hours talking to Mrs Annie Huntington and Mrs Fiona Haywood about their exceptional potagers. I also acknowledge Mr David Chase who, with Mike and Dominic Rendell, plants my entirely new potager design each spring at West Green House.

Clay and I received very practical help with research from Christine Reid and Jane and Lestocque Orman. Thanks also to Camille Wray at British Airways who made travel a pleasure.

My deepest gratitude to Maggie Perry who steered the voyage of discovery and to Clay Perry who again created camera magic. Thanks once again to Geoff Hayes for a beautifully designed book. Thanks to Helen Taylor and Julie Bostock for deciphering my manuscript, and Helen Woodhall, Senior Editor at Kyle Cathie, for coping with a long distance gardener.